GIN

Edible

Series Editor: Andrew F. Smith

EDIBLE is a revolutionary new series of books dedicated to food and drink that explores the rich history of cuisine. Each book reveals the global history and culture of one type of food or beverage.

Already published

Gin

A Global History

Lesley Jacobs Solmonson

REAKTION BOOKS

To David. The tonic to my gin.

Published by Reaktion Books Ltd
33 Great Sutton Street
London EC1V 0DX, UK
www.reaktionbooks.co.uk

First published 2012
Reprinted 2013, 2014

Printed and bound in China
by Toppan Printing Co. Ltd

British Library Cataloguing in Publication Data
Solmonson, Lesley Jacobs
Gin: a global history. – (Edible)
1. Gin--History.
I. Title II. Series
641.2´55´09-dc23

ISBN 978 1 86189 924 8

Contents

Introduction

The first use of the word 'gin' in printed English can be found in Bernard Mandeville's *The Fable of the Bees, or Private Vices, Publick Benefits* (1714):

> Nothing is more destructive, either in regard to the Health or the Vigilance and Industry of the Poor than the infamous Liquor, the name of which derived from juniper-berries in Dutch, is now, by frequent use and the Laconick spirit of the nation, from a word of middling length shrunk into a Monosyllable, Intoxicating Gin, that charms the unactive, the desperate, and crazy of either Sex . . . It is a fiery Lake that sets the Brain in Flame, burns up the Entrails, and scorches every Part within; and at the same time a Lethe of Oblivion, in which the Wretch immers'd drowns his most pinching Cares.

What Mandeville describes here so passionately is the toxic alcohol that almost crippled London during the Gin Craze of the 1700s. Surprisingly, it is this same killer gin that evolved into the classic drink of modern times.

Every spirit – be it gin, whisky, rum or brandy – has a tale to tell. Gin's story is rife with contradiction. It has been the

William Heath, *Gin: Let's Have T'other*, c. 1880s, hand-coloured etching.
Decrying the effects of gin drinking, the caption at the bottom reads
'Gin an' Glory leads to the grave as Milton ses.'

drink of both kings and commoners. It inspired the first modern drug craze in eighteenth-century London, yet London Dry gin went on to become the embodiment of sophistication in the dry Martini. In America, it was both saviour and demon – a medicinal aide in the original 'Cocktail' and a pariah during Prohibition. And, while gin is enshrined in modern bar culture, it still battles the remnants of a negative reputation, as seen in expressions like 'gin-mills', 'gin-soaked' and 'gin-joints'.

Of all the spirits, gin is quite possibly the most beloved and the most berated. Those who enjoy the juniper-based liquor often drink it to the exclusion of all others. Those who favour a different poison loudly decry gin's charms, claiming that, as one poetic barfly pronounced, 'gin tastes like Christmas trees smell.' To some extent, that piney character is gin's defining glory and its inevitable curse.

Juniper, gin's key flavouring ingredient, has been used since ancient times for its medicinal benefits. Indeed, juniper's

John Collier, *Be Here, Old and Merry Kate, and Nan, and Bess, c.* 1773, engraving. This post-Gin Craze caricature criticizes both gin-drinking and women imbibing. The woman on the left downs a goblet of gin; the woman on the right holds a punch bowl full of popular gin punch.

curative properties were so well-accepted that it was a natural, if somewhat erroneous, transition from healthful tonic to 'therapeutic' spirit. Whether used medically or recreationally, gin's singular character is determined by the juniper plant's aromatic berries, properly referred to as cones. Simply defined, then, gin is primarily a grain-based spirit, distilled with a variety of botanicals, most frequently and prominently juniper.

Yet this description is somewhat facile; gin is far more than a fragrant alcoholic beverage. Rather, it is a spyglass through which one can trace social, political and even agricultural developments. As the Mandeville passage so clearly illustrates, the story of gin is a story of discoveries. For example, while most people immediately think of Great Britain when they think of gin, its official birthplace is thirteenth-century Flanders. There, gin began life as *jenever*, the Dutch word for juniper.

Genever, the English spelling of *jenever*, is a vastly different animal from the clear, crisp liquid that most people sip in

Juniper berries, the classic botanical for flavouring gin.

Publicity card depicting the the Louis Meeùs distillery in Antwerp, c. 1900.

their gin and tonic. Being primarily flavoured with juniper, it is still considered gin by definition, but it has more in common with the malt-like sweetness of whisky.

In the 1700s, the English acquired a taste for genever, but their distillers were unable to replicate it. Consequently, during the Gin Craze which blossomed a few years after Mandeville's observations, English gin had more in common with moonshine. In the 1800s, this rough product evolved into a style known as Old Tom, which favoured botanicals – a combination of herbs, spices and other ingredients that give each gin its unique flavour profile – as well as sweetening to cater to the taste of the times.

Old Tom begat London Dry, gin's most famous incarnation. And, with London Dry as a touchstone, dynamic modern distillers from around the world are producing a remarkable range of artisan gins using exotic botanicals and experimental distillation techniques. No longer predictable in style, gin today pushes the boundaries of the standard definition. Moreover, styles once lost to the vagaries of time have been

Advertisement for Gordon's Gin, 1960s. As the key to a dry Martini, London Dry gin embodied the height of sophistication.

resurrected, exposing gin lovers – and naysayers – to an entire new world of tastes.

Gin: A Global History explores the evolution of this enigmatic beverage from its application as a medicinal tincture to a literal destroyer of men to its dynamic role in the birth of the cocktail. In the words of Lord Kinross, author of *The Kindred Spirit*, 'The story of gin is a success story – that of an ardent spirit which rose from the gutter to become the respected companion of civilized man.'

I

Gin's Medicinal Origins

Civilization begins with distillation.
William Faulkner

The history of gin is irrevocably linked to the juniper plant and its fragrant berry. In ancient times, juniper, which is part of the cypress family, was thought to be a curative for all manner of ills. Pliny the Elder mentioned it in his *Natural History*, while Aristotle claimed it was conducive to good health. The ancient Egyptians boiled juniper with frankincense, cumin and goose fat, as a treatment for headaches. The Arabs extracted the gum vernix, or resin, of the juniper tree and used it for toothache pain. In both ancient and medieval times, a concoction of sweet wine and herbs – including juniper, sage, rosemary and marjoram – was drunk as a contraceptive and to induce abortions. It was not until much later that juniper's medicinal properties were eschewed for its distinct presence as the key flavouring agent in modern gin.

Alcohol and the Ancient World

Gin's story, like that of all distilled spirits, begins with the fortuitous discovery of alcohol itself. Alcohol is a natural by-product of fermentation wherein yeasts interact with sugars. The exact date that our Neolithic forbears first fermented beverages is impossible to establish due to the lack of written records. Regardless, it was a happy accident of nature that exposed them to alcohol's unique effects and convinced them to actively produce a prehistoric brew. Indeed, residue analysed from Stone Age pottery jars found in China and Mesopotamia suggests that the containers were used to store alcoholic drinks made from a variety of agricultural products, including rice, barley and grapes. Whether the liquor was being used for medicinal, ceremonial or recreational purposes is not certain, but the bar was officially open.

Juniper, line drawing. Historically, the entire plant – bark, berries, needles and resin – was used for medicinal purposes.

Starting around 4000 BC, there is evidence through hieroglyphs and in the remains of the world's most ancient brewery in Hierakonpolis, Egypt, that our ancestors on the Nile were not teetotallers. Neither were the Greeks, although they tended toward moderation, despite often being identified with the cult of Bacchus, that lascivious lover of the vine. It was the Romans who eventually accepted Bacchus as their own and spread the cultivation of wine as far as they conquered or as far as the grape would grow, whichever came first.

Alchemy and the Middle Ages

Had our bibulous ancestors been content with wine and beer alone, we would be all the poorer for it. To our great benefit, the curiosity of Arab alchemists led to the discovery of spirits, or what we now know as hard liquor. Beer and wine are created through the fermentation of yeast to produce liquids that are no higher than approximately 15 per cent alcohol by volume (ABV). Spirits like gin are made by distilling an ethanol-containing liquid of fermented grains, fruits or vegetables. While water boils at 100°C, ethanol boils at only 78.3°C. The process of distillation discovered by the Arabs separates the ethanol from the water, creating an alcoholic vapour which can be collected. As the vapour cools, it returns to its liquid form but in a transmuted state – it is now that magical elixir known as a spirit.

While Europe was plodding along under the pall of the Dark Ages (generally recognized now as the fourth to the ninth centuries AD), the Arab alchemists were distilling with vigour. Aristotle had spoken of converting sea water into purified drinking water, but most scholars attribute the fine art of distillation to Jābir Ibn Hayyān (AD 721–815). Known in the West as

وهوذا مخلوط بآلمجز اذا صب على القروح الخبيثة والقروح المعفنة وعضة
الكلبة نهشة ذوات السموم نفع منها وقد يقطع نزف الدم العارض من

التنجه اذا اصب وهو نخن؟ النجه وقد يزد ادخال السرو النار الخارج
وقد يحقن به من كان به امعاء وقرحة خبيثة لبسط الامعا وينبغي اذا
بحقنة صاحب القرحه ان يحقن لين واذا يبسى ونعرعة قيل العلق
بالحقن وقد ينفخ لها الرز والقرح الرطبه العارضه فيه ع ع

Two doctors arguing over a patient, from an Arabic translation of Dioscorides' *De Materia Medica* (1222).

Geber, Jābir sought to discover the legendary 'quintessence', by turns considered to be a substance that could transmute base metal into gold or that was the elixir of life.

Perhaps Jābir's greatest historical contribution, at least as far as gin is concerned, was the alembic still. In the first century

17

AD, Dioscorides had described distillation in his *De Materia Medica*, and his observations of this and general herbal remedies continued to circulate throughout the world, serving as the basis for all modern pharmacopeia. Concurrently, records indicate that Maria the Jewess, an alchemist at the University of Alexandria, invented several types of stills, including an alembic. The Arabs, in particular, gathered all this knowledge for their own alchemical work.

Stemming from the Arab word *al-inbiq*, meaning 'still', the alembic is the forefather of the modern pot still, a bulb-like copper apparatus used in spirits production. Jābir perfected the process of distilling alcohol, but he had no specific use for it.

It took Al-Razi (AD 865–925, anglicized as Rhazes) to recognize that distilling alcohol could be useful as a vehicle for medicine. The product of his distillation was *aqua vitae*. Translated from the Latin as 'water of life', this elixir would be used

Hieronymus Brunschwig, *Distillation Apparatus*, 15th century, engraving.

in the coming centuries for a myriad of afflictions before finally being drunk recreationally and setting the stage for the birth of a true gin.

The work of Jābir and Al-Razi spread across Europe, reaching the Benedictine monks in Salerno, Italy. Historically, in addition to their spiritual nature, monasteries were also centres of healing where the monks experimented with and produced all sorts of medicinal tinctures. We have neither names nor exact dates, but one of these industrious monks can surely be credited with creating what Geraldine Coates, in her book *Classic Gin*, refers to as 'the first proto-gin', a juniper-based distillation for bladder and kidney problems.

Distilling went out of fashion for a few centuries until it was again chronicled by Arnaldus de Villanova, a thirteenth-century professor at the University of Montpelier and Avignon. In his *Book of Wine*, Villanova writes of the life-affirming properties of *aqua vitae* and its flavouring with an assortment of herbs and spices.

Juniper and the Reaper

It was not long before distillation left the confines of the monastery and settled quite comfortably in the homes of the nobility. Having been employed for centuries as a cure-all, juniper was often added to homemade cordials and liqueurs. However, the pleasantries of sipping a juniper-infused tonic at home were soon overshadowed by the hysteria of a populace desperate to ward off the Grim Reaper himself. The Black Death had arrived and juniper was about to play a crucial role as the 'wonder drug' of the fourteenth century.

Yersinia pestis, a bacterium spread by infected fleas on rats and later known as the bubonic plague, quickly brought

Hans Weidich, 'Neither Man or Animal is Immune from the Plague', illustration to a German edition of Petrarch's works (1532), woodcut.

Europe to its knees, killing its victims within seven days, spreading from soul to soul without discrimination, and leaving a swathe of panic in its wake. Millions died; it took Europe almost a century to recover from the devastation. Today, the plague can be effectively treated with a simple course of antibiotics. In the spring of 1348, when the plague blanketed the European continent, the inhabitants were literally defenceless.

It was a commonly – and wrongly – held belief that the sickness was spread by breathing in the noxious vapours of the disease. Thus, to combat the stench of rotting bodies and to ward off the deadly airborne poisons, people employed the aromas of juniper and its botanical siblings. Fire was the primary disinfectant against the epidemic; raging bonfires were fuelled by juniper, rosemary and incense. The brave soul who set foot outside his home did so with an herbal pomander in hand.

In 1365, John of Burgundy advised of this in his famous *Plague Treatise*:

Giovanni Grevembroch (d. 1807), *Doctor in Venice at the Time of the Plague*, watercolour.

In cold or rainy weather you should light fires in your chamber and in foggy or windy weather you should inhale aromatics every morning before leaving home . . . Later, on going to bed, shut the windows and burn juniper branches so that the smoke and scent fills the room . . . And do this as often as a foetid or bad odour can be detected in the air, and . . . it can protect against the epidemic.

The doctor of the day had no real remedies to speak of, administering herbal tinctures and elixirs with little success. He did, however, manage to cast a terrifying figure amid the chaos. In a flowing black robe, his face was covered by a freak-ishly elongated nose cone filled primarily with juniper. Looking like nothing so much as an enormous beak, this protective mask inspired the evolution of the term 'quack' for a doctor of ill repute.

In the wake of the plague, Europe's populace was reduced by almost one-half, making labour a commodity, raising wages and undermining the entire concept of feudalism. As explained by Iain Gately in his book *Drink*, the emerging workforce flooded from the countryside to the towns, bring-ing with it a thirst that demanded commercial-scale liquor production. This new free-market economy spawned an equally new concept of leisure time, allowing the public drinking house to evolve and thrive.

One could say that, indirectly, gin is indebted to the plague for its long-term evolution. For without the rise of commercially made alcohol, free-market competition and the multitudes of new drinking establishments, gin – indeed alcohol collectively – would never have achieved its foothold in Western culture.

2

Genever in the Low Countries

Des zeemans allerbest compas is een gevuld Genever-Glas.
A sailor's best working compass is a glass completely
filled with genever.

Dutch saying

Before there was gin, there was genever. First distilled primarily in what would become Holland and Belgium, genever is the gin that even gin drinkers do not know. Pronounced 'YUH-nee-vur', the word means, quite simply, juniper. Eventually, the British would anglicize the word to 'geneva' (no relation to the Swiss city) and then to the more prosaic 'gin'. However, to call genever 'Dutch gin', as it is often labelled, not only insults both products, but also proves to be remarkably incorrect. In fact, gin and genever are less brother and sister than they are kissing cousins. Where modern gin is essentially flavoured vodka, genever is headier stuff, having more in common with fine whisky than the clear-coloured aromatics of English gin. It was this whisky-like spirit that seduced British soldiers after the Fall of Antwerp, in what is now Belgium. And it was the adulterated, poor man's version of this fine drink that brought London to its knees during the Gin Craze of the eighteenth century.

Juniper Spirits

Genever has a long history in the Low Countries, a geo-political term that comprises the low-lying delta formed by the Meuse, Scheldt and Rhine rivers. Today, this region includes the Netherlands, Belgium, Luxembourg, portions of northern France (French Flanders) and parts of Germany.

Around AD 1000, the region was little more than a feudal society of kings, clergy, a few free men and many serfs living in small villages without centralized rule. The next three centuries saw a profound period of change characterized by the rise of urban centres and more defined governance. In 1369, Philip the Bold, Duke of Burgundy, married Margaret III, Countess of Flanders, beginning the era of Burgundian Rule, which ended when the Spanish Habsburgs came to govern the Low Countries in 1482.

While in power, Philip had hoped to centralize the region. This continued vision, coupled with an emerging distaste for Habsburg rule, engendered a burgeoning sense of nationalism that would eventually unite the Low Countries politically, geographically and in their taste for genever.

In the early Middle Ages, the juniper destined to be used in genever was already a fixture on the shelves of European apothecary shops. The first major mention in printed Dutch of juniper-based tonics can be found in *Der Naturen Bloeme* ('The Flower of Nature'), written in 1269 by Jacob van Maerlant, the greatest Flemish poet of the era. The work is a free-form, twelve-volume translation of *Liber de Natura Rerum*, a mid-thirteenth-century natural history by Thomas of Cantimpré. Along with chapters about 'the monstrous races' (Cyclops, pygmies and so on) and sea monsters (*Canis marinus* or the 'sea-dog'), van Maerlant illuminated more useful information. It is in chapter Eight, entitled *Gewone Bomen*, or 'Ordinary

Page from Jacob van Maerlant, *Der Naturen Bloeme* ('The Flower of Nature') (1269).

Trees', that we find the passage that essentially serves as the basis for all genever in the Low Countries:

The juniper bush is an evergreen.

Hot and dry of manner, the working of juniper is natural, releasing and removing bad spirits.
He who suffers from stomach pains should cook juniper berries in rain water.
He who suffers from cramps should cook juniper berries in wine to alleviate the pain.

From this tree we make an oil with large potential/possibilities.
Dry the wood in the air, then put it in a pot, filling it for one-third, then another one on top, then another one on top.
Seal the pots and heat them, and the resulting oil can be cooled in a pot in the earth.

This (oil) is good against ailments, stomach cramps, against mortal pain and can be mixed into food.

Van Maerlant's work is dissected by professor and Nationaal Jenevermuseum Hasselt chairman Eric Van Schoonenberghe in his authoritative book *Jenever in de Lage Landen* (1996). Van Schoonenberghe notes that the above passage uses the same pot-to-pot distilling process originally recorded by Dioscorides in the first century. Dioscorides' terminology – *distillatio per descensum* – is defined by a distilling system that has the lowest pot cooled in the earth. Notably, van Maerlant's work suggests an awareness of ancient distillation techniques.

When the Plague broke out in the Low Countries in 1349, juniper was the familiar, albeit ineffective, panacea. Little more than a century later, in 1497, Amsterdam tax records list an excise duty being levied on what was known as *brandewijn*, or 'burned wine'. This is important insomuch as 'burned wine' is the result of distilling wine – that is, brandy – and a tax on said spirit suggests that it was being used recreationally. A similar tax was first levied in Antwerp in 1551.

Toward the end of the 1400s, a Middle Dutch manuscript for making 'burned wine' included a recipe for distilling *aqua vitae*, further suggesting that brandy had become a cooking staple, not just a medicinal one. The text also offers up a recipe using modern gin's familiar botanicals, including nutmeg, ginger, galangal, grains of paradise, peppers, cloves, cinnamon and cardamom. Specifically stating that only distilled wine may be used as a base, this is one of the first references to a recreational spirit redistilled with botanicals.

In the year 1552, the city of Antwerp puts us one step closer to 'real' genever. The publication of Philippus Hermanni's *Een Constelijck Distilleer Boek* contains the first reference to a recreational juniper berry spirit. Hermanni dubs it *geneverbessenwater*, Dutch for 'juniper berry water'.

At this point, however, juniper was still being combined with distilled wine, not the traditional grain of genever or gin. Only a few decades later, we find the first citation of distilling grain in Casper Jansz.'s *A Guide to Distilling* (1582), which describes corn brandy-wine – that is, grain alcohol – as 'in aroma and taste almost the same as brandy-wine . . . (it is) not only named brandywine but also drunk and paid for as brandywine.'

Grain Spirits

The use of grain came about for several reasons. Paintings by Pieter Brueghel the Elder (1525/30–1569) such as *Hunters in the Snow* and *Winter Landscape with a Birdtrap* testify to the chilling northern climate brought on by the nascent Little Ice Age. During this period, winters were exceedingly harsh and long, while spring and summer months tended toward cooler temperatures. Grapes struggled in such conditions, while the hardier grains like rye and barley could be grown locally and stored more easily. In addition, frequent trade blockades with wine-producing nations like Spain and Italy made wine difficult to obtain and, if obtainable, imported at prohibitive costs. It comes as no surprise then that ordinary citizens turned to distilling more readily available ingredients to produce mead, beer and brandy made from both of the latter.

The extreme popularity of grain brandy in the southern Low Countries resulted in a 1601 edict from Archduke Albert, the ruling Habsburg. In it, he prohibited the production and

Postcard advertising Bols, *c.* 1915. Note the date of establishment as 1575.

Clay bottles, *c.* 1890–1935. This was the typical bottling of the era, which has long since been replaced by glass.

sale of brandy, suggesting that grain would be better used for making bread than for distilling. As with all prohibitions, the laws were not completely respected and, in fact, led to an exodus of Flemish distillers – many had already fled in 1568 at the start of the Eighty Years War – to other parts of Europe. They took with them their knowledge; from 1500 to 1700, hundreds of distillers set up shop in the future Netherlands, France and Germany.

During this era, the Dutch East India Company (Vereenigde Oost-Indische Compagnie or VOC) erupted onto the world scene, changing the face of commerce. The Dutch had always been known for travelling extensively, acquiring and spreading knowledge. They were also superb businessmen and, by the end of the sixteenth century, they had further incentives to venture across the globe. While they controlled trade routes

Genever glasses, *c.* 1920–40. The Netherlands has built an entire drink culture around genever, including specially shaped glasses for the spirit.

in the Baltic and the North Sea, they had yet to access the immensely profitable Asian spice routes held by the Portuguese.

The Dutch had little respect for the Portuguese, whose careless business practices caused the price of spices like pepper – for which demand was fixed – to escalate as demand could not be met. Further, the Portuguese shared a king with Catholic Spain, with whom the Protestant Dutch were at war. Portugal thus made a tempting military target. Spurred by these various factors, in 1602 the States-General of the Netherlands granted the VOC a 21-year monopoly in Asia and created the first multinational corporation in the process. While optimizing a trade monopoly – from the Cape of Good Hope to Japan – that conveniently fed into their need for a spiced beverage called genever, the VOC spread its roughly 30,000 employees around the globe, and with them went the juniper-based spirit.

Around 1730, genever was shipped with herbs known as *lepelblad*, or 'scurvy-grass', to prevent the then-deadly affliction of scurvy. Furthermore, from 1742 on the Chamber Amsterdam of the VOC ordered genever to replace *korenbrandewijn*, which had been used since the 1600s, because the juniper berries used in genever were considered healthful. Even as late as 1863, a medical directive considered genever rations to be 'effective medicine'.

Where the VOC went, Dutch troops followed, assisting in settlement and peace-keeping. In *Fugitive Dreams: An Anthology of Dutch Colonial Literature* (1998), we find passages to support the constant and essential presence of genever in the military as late as the nineteenth century:

> Drinking was officially sanctioned by the Dutch military authorities, as it was also by the British, although the Dutch were far more generous in their allotments. Recruits received a ration of 'jenever', or Dutch gin, as soon as they had been quartered in the Harderwijk depot. Liquor was also made available while the troops were at sea.

An order issued in 1864 stipulated that on board chartered ships, gin was to be distributed as follows: 'for European, African, and Ambonese non-commissioned officers and troops, and for European women: in the morning 0.075 Dutch *kan* of jenever; in the afternoon 0.075 *kan* jenever; in the evening 0.075 *kan* jenever.' A *kan* was about a litre, hence this was equivalent to a ration of a quarter-cup three times daily.

In Atjeh, during the 1880s, a sergeant or other NCO walked along the lines of men standing in formation and poured a glass of gin from a square, green bottle. The soldier that the glass was handed to had to down it with one gulp and pass it on to the next man.

Fugitive Dreams also notes that a variety of creative terms evolved for genever. These included *oorlam*, from the Malay phrase meaning 'a person who arrived a long time ago', 'parrot soup' (*papegaaiensoep*), a 'fat head' (*dikkop*), 'hopping water' (*huppelwater*), 'seawater' (*zeewater*), 'straight up and down' (*recht op en neer*) and a 'bite of pea soup' (*hap snert*).

Another passage suggests that perhaps the Dutch took their commitment to genever a bit too seriously:

> To the Indonesian population, drunkenness (*mabok*) became synonymous with being a Dutchman. A native woman considered herself lucky if she found a European man who was not *mabok* all the time when off duty, and who did not love the 'square lout' (*vierkante lummel*, or genever bottle) above anything else.

As the VOC brought spices back to Holland, it spread genever across the globe as far as Asia and West Africa. When the VOC finally went bankrupt and closed its doors in 1799, Dutch entrepreneurs took over the shipment of genever to the various Dutch colonies, as well as Britain, France and the Americas.

The Myth of Doctor Sylvius

The seventeenth century was the Netherlands' golden age. While the Dutch East India Company was colonizing the far reaches of the globe, artists such as Rembrandt were painting in Amsterdam. Along with art and trade, medicine was also evolving. And it is at this point in time that we meet Dr Franciscus Sylvius, who was making juniper-laced tonics from 1658 to 1672 at the University of Leiden. It has been claimed –

quite erroneously – that the good doctor is 'the Father of Dutch Gin'. While he was indeed serving up genever as a medicine for kidney complaints and for the tropical fever attacking Dutch settlers in the East Indies, a true inventor he was not. Given the fact that so many histories and papers give Sylvius such important credit, it is worth taking the time to debunk the mythology.

The Nationaal Jenevermuseum Hasselt in Belgium states unequivocally that genever was created in the lowlands of Flanders in the thirteenth century. Their claim is given credence by commentary in *Jenever in de Lange Landen*. Therein, author Eric Van Schoonenberghe thoroughly dissects the Sylvius myth, explaining that the dates simply do not add up.

Cornelius van Dalen, *Dr Franciscus Sylvius*, 1659, engraving. Erroneously named 'the Father of Dutch Gin, Sylvius is wrongly credited with inventing genever.

FRANCISCUS DELEBOE SYLVIUS, MEDICINÆ PRACTICÆ IN ACADEMIA LUGDUNO-BATAVA PROFESSOR.

In a 1992 speech, the late archivist from Bols, Holland's first and leading genever manufacturer, agreed with Van Schoon-enberghe's conclusions.

When Sylvius was born in 1614, corn brandy (*korenbran-dewijn*) was already being labelled and taxed as such, and had been since 1608. Corn brandy was, of course, grain-based liquor needing only an extra distillation with juniper berries to transform it into genever. (We should recall that juniper-infused brandy had already been mentioned in Hermanni's *Een Constelijck Distilleer Boek*.) Prior to Sylvius's time at Leiden, he served as a plague doctor from 1655 to 1656, during which time he likely employed juniper-based elixirs. However, these had been used since the fourteenth-century plague outbreak and before. Further, during his fourteen-year term as a professor at Leiden, none of his research or papers contains a reference to genever and he was only cited once for distilling-related expertise.

Much more evidence exists that the groundwork was laid for genever before Sylvius was born. In 1609, in a medieval English cookbook grandly titled *Delightes for ladies: to adorn their persons, tables, closets, and distillatories with beauties, banquets, per-fumes, and waters*, author Sir Hugh Platt describes 'Spirits of Spices'. In these spirits, one should 'distill with a gentle heat . . . the strong and sweet water where you have drawn oil of cloves, mace, nutmeg, juniper, rosemary, &c.' It almost reads like a modern gin formula. Likewise, the Count de Morret, son of Henry iv of France, had perfected the making of juniper-flavoured wine around this time.

And, in 1623, when Sylvius was just a lad of nine, we find what is thought to be the first printed reference to genever as a recreational drink, suggesting quite clearly that it was already in existence. In Act 1, Scene 1 of Philip Massinger's Jacob-ean tragedy *The Duke of Milan*, a character named Graccho mentions 'geneva spirit'. Incidentally, it is interesting to note that Massinger was English; by this time, London was already playing host to 6,000 Flemish Protestants who had fled Antwerp in 1570 and had clearly brought their taste for genever – 'geneva spirit' – with them.

Genever Production Evolves

The widespread availability of genever in the Low Countries took time to develop. Government subsidies, plentiful grain and public demand were all factors in its production. In the area that would become Belgium, the beverage languished after Archduke Albert's 1601 edict, which sent so many Flemish distillers fleeing for their livelihood. Hasselt, which belonged to the domain of the Prince Bishop of Liège until 1795, was the only town that evaded the edict and continued to produce genever. In fact, production exploded when the city was occupied by a Dutch garrison from 1675 to 1681. Today, Hasselt genever is more diversely flavoured than any other in the country due to this Dutch influence.

Under Austrian rule from 1713 to 1794, the distillation of grain-based brandy was again encouraged in the south, but less for the brandy than the draff (in Dutch, *draf*), the residue that settled in the still after the first distillation of fermented mash. The draff was used to fatten up cattle and the grain brandy produced, though usually not flavoured with juniper, was still loosely, if not quite correctly, referred to as genever. Even in the present day, some eastern Flemish genevers do not contain juniper.

In the nineteenth century, genever production was at its height thanks to the Industrial Revolution and a Frenchman by the name of Jean-Baptiste Cellier Blumenthal. In 1813, Cellier

Blumenthal, who was a good friend of Belgian King Leopold, patented the first vertical continuous distillation column. King Leopold had widespread sugar beet farms and, by the end of the 1800s, sugar beet was used to distil neutral alcohol for genever using Cellier Blumenthal's apparatus. The result was an inferior product that lost its rich grain character.

Traditional distillers fought back by labelling their genever as being made according to the *vieux système*, or the 'old method', using grain. Unfortunately, many agricultural distillers were forced out of business due to new excise duties and the competition from large-scale, industrial distilleries. Mass production would eventually be the undoing of Belgian genever.

In stark contrast to Belgium's struggling industry, the Netherlands' genever culture flourished. For instance, in 1700, there were only 37 distilleries in the Schiedam area; by 1800, there were 250.

Historically, Bols is the oldest and most influential of all the Dutch genever companies. Originally named Bulsius, the

Bols distillery in Amsterdam. By 1652, the original *Lootsje* ('little shed') had been replaced with these grand stone buildings. The affectionate moniker remained.

The director of Bols posing before stills and coolers, *c.* 1904.

Flemish Bols family escaped religious persecution and fled to Cologne. Led by Lucas Bols, they were in Cologne when the Protestant Flemish community there began distilling brandy from corn. With this knowledge, the Bols family immigrated to Amsterdam. Just outside the city, they set up a distillery in a woodshed, dubbing it *'t Lootsje* ('the little shed'). By 1664, Bols received a spirits licence and started production of genever. It is probably no small coincidence that the van Dale dictionary, Holland's equivalent of the *Oxford English Dictionary*, first included the word 'genever' in 1672.

Part of Bols' success can be linked to the Dutch East India Company. VOC archives note that, from 1680 to 1719, Bols was the exclusive supplier of 'fine waters' to the VOC's powerful inner circle of the Seventeen Gentlemen ('Heeren XVII'), who served as the board of directors for the organization. With this privilege came opportunity. Lucas Bols' position entitled him

Belgian poster advising Temperance and published by the Liberal People's Party (Liberale Volkspartij), *c.* 1900s. 'Drunkenness causes misery and premature death. Citizens of all classes, abstain from liquor.'

to a large number of shares in the VOC from 1679 on; this, in turn, gained him prime access to the herbs and spices that the colonial trade was bringing back to Amsterdam. In 1820, when the company introduced a new genever recipe, it is likely that these exotic ingredients played a major role.

The Bols family set the stage for the future crop of genever distillers. DeKuyper, established in 1695, began genever production in 1729. By the nineteenth century, they concentrated on export sales to Great Britain and her colonies. Other companies, such as Rutte, followed.

In both nineteenth-century Holland and Belgium, genever consumption was prodigious, to say the least. Indeed, Michael Wintle's *An Economic and Social History of the Netherlands, 1800–1920* (2000), notes that, in the early 1830s alone, approximately 10 litres of 50 per cent pure alcohol was drunk each year per head of population. The numbers were similar in Belgium and, as might be expected, Temperance movements followed in both countries.

Louis Meeùs publicity card, c. 1934.

Dutch and Belgian genever experienced their share of public relations issues. In Belgium, genever became known as 'the poor man's drink', to its great detriment. In Holland, it was the frequent tipple of unskilled labourers, who were dubbed the 'genever-drinking classes' by Dutch liberal politician Samuel van Houten (1837–1930). Despite this name-calling, genever managed to shed this negative image and emerge unscathed in the Netherlands.

In the 1700s and 1800s, genever became quite popular in Great Britain and America, the former's upper classes embracing the spirit and the latter's using it in pre-Prohibition cocktails. Today, despite many bumps in the road, genever is considered the national drink of both the Netherlands and Belgium. More importantly, it can lay claim to being the 'original' gin, giving birth to a spirit and a cocktail culture that changed the world.

3

Gin in Britain
The Gin Craze

Drunk for a penny,
Dead drunk for two,
Clean straw for nothing.
Eighteenth-century dram shop sign

Indirectly, it was Robert Dudley, first Earl of Leicester, who brought gin to England. Dudley was a strong supporter of the Protestant cause, so much so that when the Dutch rebelled against Spanish Habsburg rule in 1585, he led the English campaign to the Netherlands. While the Earl enjoyed the comforts of his station, his soldiers faced the Spanish forces, one of the most well-outfitted and skilled armies in Europe. It comes as no surprise that mass desertions followed. While Dudley failed in his military role, for our story, he was a hero: he sent his men home with a taste for genever. A similar scene would occur when troops returned from the Thirty Years War (1618–48). However, instead of deserting, they would gulp a dram of genever, which fortified them for battle, thus earning genever the moniker 'Dutch Courage'.

In Dudley's time, English distillers were starting to dabble with juniper as a flavouring for spirits. Around 1570,

E. Heemskerck, *A Satire on Gin-drinking, c.* 1770s, engraving. One in a series of grotesques, this image condemns the gin sellers and turns the consumers into 'animals'.

'strong water' shops specializing in variously flavoured *aqua vitae* – aniseed was quite popular – started popping up around the country, a foreshadowing of the dram shops and gin palaces of the next two centuries.

By 1600, there were 200 of these 'houses' distilling in London. In 1638, the Worshipful Company of Distillers, one of London's many livery companies, was incorporated by Royal Charter to regulate the production of spirits. And just five years later, the House of Lords thought spirits were enough of

The coat of arms of the Worshipful Company of Distillers, one of the Livery Companies of the City of London, that regulated the production of spirits.

DROP AS RAIN · DISTIL · AS DEW

a revenue source to tax them at eight pence on every gallon (4.54 litres) imported, made or distilled within England.

Taxation did nothing to slow production, although it is likely that *aqua vitae*'s identity suffered from a conflict in perception. On the one hand, people were drinking it for sport and falling down drunk, since the alcoholic proof of 'strong waters' far outstripped the strength of their usual beer or ale. On the other, medicinal tonics were still the rage. In Book II of *The Art of Distillation* (1653), John French, Doctor of Physick, described 'an excellent water against the Stones in the Kidneys', which called for bruised juniper berries, 'venice turpentine' and spring water.

In all likelihood, it was this or a similar recipe that was mentioned as a curative in *The Diary of Samuel Pepys*. On 10 October 1663, Pepys complained that he was 'Up, and not in any good ease yet, but had pain in making water.' He was then advised to take some 'strong water made of juniper', which cured his condition.

Towards the end of the seventeenth century, hard liquor faced some competition from an assortment of imported hot beverages. The first coffee house opened in London in 1650; in 1657, the first chocolate house appeared; and tea was first served in a London coffee house around the same time. Still, demand was high for spirits of all kinds; Dutch genever and French brandy were the choices of the wealthy, leaving the hoi polloi with rotgut gin, now being produced in large, unmonitored quantities.

Jessica Warner, in her article 'The Naturalization of Beer and Gin in Early Modern England' (1997), suggests that there were three factors necessary for this deadly gin – a far cry from true genever – to be embraced by the working poor. First, the beverage needed to be affordable, more so than

John French, woodcut illustration from *The Art of Distillation* (1653).

the national beverages of beer and ale. Second, it needed to offer 'a movement in either taste or potency'. The term 'taste' here is defined as 'sheer novelty', given that the diet of the poor was quite dismal (often spoiled meat, stale vegetables and bread coloured with alum and chalk to make it look white). Moreover, the lower classes always sought to emulate their more fortunate superiors, who drank fine genever. The final, crucial factor was that gin needed to be produced locally, which would ensure lower distilling costs and uninterrupted availability.

The stars aligned for all these factors in 1688. This was the year of the Glorious Revolution, when the Dutch-born William of Orange overthrew his Catholic, brandy-drinking, French-sympathizing father-in-law King James ii and took the throne of England for himself and his wife Mary ii. William's legacy is far-reaching, but in the history of gin, only one thing is of consequence. William was a Protestant gin drinker from Holland.

Gin Mania

Blue Ruin, Ladies' Delight, Cuckold's Comfort. The sobriquets for the eighteenth-century drug of choice were legion. Never before had England been so mesmerized by a beverage; never again would the city of London be as consistently intoxicated as it was between 1720 and 1751. Indeed, from 1684 to 1710, while beer production fell by 12 per cent and strong beer by 22.5 per cent, gin production rose by 400 per cent.

Some scholars have likened the Gin Craze, as it has become known, to the crack epidemic in 1980s America. Both do share similarities with addiction, in this case, being mostly a phenomenon of the urban poor. However, the Gin Craze is unique in that it was, as Jessica Warner points out, 'the first modern drug scare' and can be used as a model for dissecting the causes of and solutions to addiction.

To understand this madness, we have to understand eighteenth-century London. Here was a city on the brink of modernity, but not yet truly modern. Immigrants flocked to the city, adding diversity but contributing to overcrowding and fuelling xenophobia. Demand for labour meant higher wages; despite their lowly status, the poor had a disposable income of sorts (as in the Middle Ages) and were eager to spend it. Further, London herself was quickly dividing into industrial and residential zones. The urban sprawl made for difficult policing; officers of the law were volunteers and the Excise Office was the only structured overseer. Causing additional strife was the omnipresent division of the classes, with the rich ensconced in luxury and the working poor confined to a squalid, sickly existence.

At this point, it is worth noting that many present-day historians have begun to dispute the actual 'craze' itself. True, the poor were indeed alcoholics of epic proportions, but the English had always been keen on drink. Despite its novelty, gin, in and of itself, was not to blame. Rather, the physical and psychological effects of poverty led to excessive consumption. Gin was readily available and very cheap; the poor merely found solace where they could.

As for King William, he did not intend to make his subjects into dipsomaniacs. Long an enemy of France, William sought to deprive the Gallic war machine of funds; at the same time, he knew he needed to find revenue streams for Britain's own continuing war efforts.

Parliament, which was composed of wealthy landowners, had its own agenda of finding outlets for its members' excess grain. Thus it was that in 1689 imports of all French spirits were banned. Subsequently in 1690 the Distilling Act dissolved the distillers' monopoly on production, raising duties on domestic spirits, while allowing anyone to make them. Finally, in 1720 the Mutiny Act offered the public an enticing piece of legislation. If a citizen distilled spirits, he was exempt from billeting soldiers in his home. It was not a difficult choice. To say that these factors encouraged local gin production is putting it lightly. Figures and dates vary by small degrees depending upon the source, but the rough consensus for gin's rise in production and consumption is as follows:

c. 1690: All of England produces approximately half a million imperial gallons of gin per annum.

1694: Beer is heavily taxed, and gin is cheaper to drink.

1720: The Mutiny Act creates a surplus of 'distillers'.

c. 1730: The number of gin shops in London equals or exceeds 7,000. One in every three public houses sells gin.

c. 1733: London alone produces eleven million gallons of legal gin, enough for fourteen gallons per person per annum.

Bear in mind that these numbers are based on a London population of roughly 600,000 people. It is easy to understand why at any given time one out of every four residents – essentially all of the city's poor – was completely and utterly incoherent.

The upper classes did not take kindly to this uninhibited rabble. Mass marketing had taken Dutch genever, which was a civilized drink of the King's court, and offered its high-street cousin to the lower classes, who revelled in their new equality. Women and men drank side by side in dram shops;

women even became proprietors. Unlike beer and ale, which provided potable nourishment and energy for work, this new English gin offered no bodily benefits, unless one counted the blissful oblivion of intoxication. It was enough to make any self-respecting aristocrat quake as the existing social order unravelled before his eyes.

In some ways, the rich were partly to blame for the madness. As Daniel Defoe observed in *A Brief Case of the Distillers* (1726), 'It seems to me (that the poor) have done . . . even what their superiors have seemed to lead them into just now, by general example.' King William, too, carries some of the burden as his dissolving of the distillers' monopoly ensured that anyone, no matter how unscrupulous, could make gin.

Equally problematic was the quality of the gin itself. The malt-like complexity of genever was far too challenging for local distillers. Instead of employing Dutch techniques, they used low-quality grain to produce neutral spirits which were cut with substances like oil of turpentine, oil of vitriol (sulphuric acid) and alum. Then, to mask the foul flavour, the gin was enhanced with ingredients including sugar, lime water and rosewater.

At approximately 160 proof, this potent brew was obscenely high in alcohol, compared to today's average of 80 proof. One shot of 160 proof spirits was certainly not deadly. Unfortunately, the gin drinkers of the eighteenth century were not just sipping gin and tonics. In some cases, they were consuming over half a litre a day of hard liquor whose quality can be likened to moonshine. A tankard of ale had become a tankard of gin.

Moreover, eighteenth-century men and women were not the size of their modern counterparts; men averaged approximately 5'6" (168 cm), while women were diminutive at 5'1" (155 cm). Nor was their poor diet nutritionally conducive to balancing their alcohol intake. High proof, lack of nutrition and small size were all ingredients in a recipe for excess.

Drunkenness in and of itself was not the problem. In the seventeenth and eighteenth centuries, drunken behaviour was not viewed with the same stigma as it is in modern times. Indeed, the rich frequently drank to excess. In *A Foreign View of England in the Reigns of George I and George II* (1902), French author César de Saussure claims that Queen Anne, who took the throne in 1702 after William's death, 'was often called "*Boutique d'Eau-de-Vie*" [essentially 'dram shop'] because of her well-known liking for the bottle and spirituous liquors'.

While the rich drank for sport, the poor drank to forget their sordid existence, and drinking often led to grave misdeeds. Transcripts from England's court of record, the Old Bailey, frequently mention gin's damning influence. Throughout the accounts, there are references to the manner in which the various offenders 'haunted the Geneva Shops' or had 'drunk too liberally of Geneva' or requested 'a Quartern of Gin'. The eighteenth-century dram shop slogan 'drunk for a penny, dead drunk for two, clean straw for nothing' illustrates the enthusiasm of the masses toward consumption and the eagerness of suppliers to provide it.

Further, a pattern emerges wherein many of the crimes committed began in a gin shop, thus reinforcing the belief of the period that gin was a breeder of wickedness. One record in the Ordinary's Accounts, which summed up the confessions and dying words of the convicted, told of Benjamin Loveday, aged seventeen:

> He was a constant Drinker of Geneva, and in little Shops he met with all the worst of Company, Whores, Thieves, &c. who never had a good Advice to give him, but still the Worst, which tended to his utter Ruin

and Destruction. He own'd, that he was a most wicked, prof-ligate, debauch'd Boy.

Loveday was charged with extortion, but pleaded his innocence, despite admitting to his drunken ways. He was found guilty and executed on 9 October 1732.

In the infamous case of Judith Defour, the accused freely admitted her guilt and, in doing so, eloquently exposed in the reformers' minds how gin was destroying the fairer sex and killing the nation's children. On 27 February 1734, Defour was indicted for the murder of her daughter Mary, who was strangled and left naked in a ditch. On giving evidence, John Wolveridge claimed that Defour confessed the deed to him thus:

> On Sunday night we took the Child into the Fields, and stripp'd it, and ty'd a Linen Handkerchief hard about its Neck to keep it from crying, and then laid it in a Ditch. After that, we went together, and sold the Coat and Stay for a Shilling, and the Petticoat and Stockings for a Groat. We parted the Money, and join'd for a Quartern of Gin.

So as gin fever swept through the bleak back alleys and lanes of the city, the ruling class experienced an almost pathologically blind desire to maintain the semi-feudal status quo of their world. Neither the government nor the wealthy were in favour of abstinence; rather, they favoured control — of the liquor and, consequently, of the masses.

From 1729 to 1751, Parliament passed eight Gin Acts, which levied taxes on Mother Gin, charged licencing fees to gin-sellers, and rewarded informers. The most notorious of these laws was the Gin Act of 1736. The law was pushed

To the Mortal Memory of Madam Geneva, 1736, engraving. In response to the
Gin Acts, various artists comically mourned gin's regulation.

through Parliament by Sir Joseph Jekyll, whose abhorrence of drunkenness fuelled his campaign. The text of the Act raised licence fees on retailing gin to an astronomical £50, created new fines for home distilling and offered £5 to informers. Sir Robert Walpole, however, opposed the law, claiming that it would do more harm than good.

The day before the law went into effect, rioting crowds used their last pennies to buy gin. On 29 September 1736, the date the Act was to be enforced, copies of an engraving entitled *The Funeral Procession of Madam Geneva* were sold. Beneath the print, a poem lamented:

The Lamentable Fall of Madam Geneva, 1736, engraving.

No dram to lift their spirits up,
Cheap Cordial for the Poors Relief!
One half Penny cou'd chace their Grief;
Two for a Penny might be Jolly,
A Quartern chear'd both John & Dolly.

Along with 'funerals' and gin-shop signs draped in black mourning cloths, there were ballads and even plays of mourning. One such piece was titled *The Deposing and Death of Queen Gin* by 'Juniper Jack, a Distiller's Apprentice, just turn'd Poet'. In it, 'Queen Gin' intones 'The Day, my Friends, the fatal Day is come'; the Mob replies 'Liberty, Property, and *Gin* for ever'.

Amid the protests both comic and tragic, Walpole's warning proved to be correct; the law was unenforceable and only encouraged crime. After a brief dip in gin sales and consumption, illicit sales of 'Parliamentary Brandy' increased as distillers hawked their wares under new names like 'Make Shift' or 'Colic Waters'; chemists sometimes even bottled them in medicinal vials.

Sometime in this period, gin also became known as 'Old Tom'. The nickname can reputedly be traced to an enterprising informer turned illegal gin-seller by the name of Captain Dudley Bradstreet. Seeing the potential in bootleg gin, Bradstreet set up shop, placing a sign of an 'old tom' cat in his window. Beneath it, a slot accepted coins and dispensed gin. Eager consumers whispered 'puss' and the seller replied 'mew' to confirm that gin was to be had. One could say that Bradstreet created the first speakeasy; the practice was duplicated all around London.

In 1737, a new Act sought to reward informers even further, the result being that they were routinely attacked by street mobs. A subsequent 1738 Act made it a crime to attack an informer. In 1743 and 1747, England was embroiled in the

War of Austrian Succession, and Parliament targeted gin once again, less for moral reasons than to raise war funds.

By 1750, the number of licensed gin retailers was close to 29,000. So-called reformers continued to blame gin for everything from poverty itself to the undermining of the workforce to promiscuity and the spread of syphilis. One of the more egregious claims was the unsubstantiated link between gin consumption and the inordinate number of childhood deaths. In point of fact, these deaths could just as easily have been – and most likely were – caused by poor living conditions and disease. Despite the lack of tangible proof, Isaac Maddox, the well-respected bishop of Worcester, went so far as to suggest that gin was literally killing England's babies and, therefore, its future soldiers and workers.

Maddox was in league with Henry Fielding, author of *Tom Jones* as well as a Westminster magistrate and Chair of the Westminster Quarter Sessions. In *An Enquiry into the Causes of the Late Increase of Robbers* (1751), Fielding blamed 'that poison called gin' for the rise in crime and claimed that it was

> the principal sustenance (if it may be so called) of more than a hundred thousand people in this metropolis. Many of these wretches there are who swallow pints of this poison within the twenty-four hours: the dreadful effects of which I have the misfortune everyday to see, and to smell too.

He concluded by offering that, 'Should the drinking of this poison be continued in its present height during the next twenty years, there will be by that time few of the common people left to drink it.' Fielding's concerns were reflected in the spread of gin consumption to the provinces, suggesting that the London epidemic might soon become that of the entire nation.

William Hogarth, *Beer Street*, 1751, engraving.

Fellow crusader William Hogarth had joined the attack as well, producing two 'satirical prints' only a month before his friend Fielding published his *Enquiry*. Hogarth's *Gin Lane* and *Beer Street* remain to this day vivid examples of how the two drinks were viewed. *Beer Street* celebrates boisterous, well-fed citizens, gleefully clutching tankards of ale. Of this scene, Hogarth remarked that 'all is joyous and thriving. Industry and jollity go hand in hand.'

55

In bleak contrast, the engraving *Gin Lane* features an intoxicated, syphilitic mother mindlessly dropping her child off a staircase while surrounded by listless, skeletal souls seeking solace in gin. Hogarth summed up the message of the picture thus: 'Idleness, poverty, misery, and distress, which drives even to madness and death, are the only objects that are to be seen.'

Hogarth's friend the Reverend James Townley composed poems for each etching. For *Beer Street*, he described beer as the

William Hogarth, *Gin Lane*, 1751, engraving.

'happy produce of our Isle, Can sinewy Strength impart'. In contrast, his scathing poem accompanying *Gin Lane* reflected the view of all the reformers when it accused:

Gin curs'd Fiend, with Fury fraught,
Makes human Race a Prey,
It enters by a deadly Draught,
And steals our Life away.

The combination of imagery and poetry hit home for many. In June of 1751 the final Gin Act was passed without a hiccup. While the prior Gin Acts had the taint of class snobbery and opportunistic taxation, the 1751 law fed off the public's fear of crime, suggesting that if the cause of crime (gin) was taken away, then crime itself would dissipate. Excises on spirits were raised by more than 50 per cent, while distillers and street vendors were forbidden to sell the product. Mother Gin did not stand a chance.

Ironically, the law came too late. Gin consumption had started to fall on its own, perhaps because the novelty had worn off, but more likely because the second half of the century saw a profound drop in wages. Likewise, rum had made a name for itself by this time, having been embraced by the British navy's enlisted men, starting in the late seventeenth century. Further, the brewing industry had launched a counterattack of its own with a new product called porter. First developed around 1722, porter was a strong, bitter, dense beer that required long maturing, but could be produced in hotter weather than light beers. It first gained popularity among London porters, thus resulting in its name.

In 1756 a major crop failure led Parliament to ban the use of domestic grains for distilled spirits. From 1760 until the end of the century, the government continued to levy taxes

The Funeral Procession of Madam Geneva, a mock funeral procession held in St Giles, London, 1751, engraving.

on spirits, but ended up encouraging smuggling instead. Gin had lost its stranglehold over the populace but, on the dawn of the Industrial Revolution, Madam Geneva was destined to walk the streets of London Town once again.

4
Gin in Britain: Colonialism, Gin Palaces, London Dry

Gin was mother's milk to her.

G. B. Shaw, *Pygmalion*

Historically, the words 'Britain' and 'Empire' are synonymous. As the saying goes, there was a time when the sun never set on the British Empire. With Empire came two elements key to gin consumption: a military whose men needed alcoholic succour and a contingent of expatriates eager to recreate the civility of home.

Britain had always been a sea power, ever hungry for conquest and discovery. During the sixteenth-century reign of Henry VIII, the Navy Royal was created. Nutrient-rich beer rations were traditional and necessary as the job of a sailor was both brutally backbreaking and incredibly monotonous. Alcohol made all concerned more pleasant.

In the eighteenth century, the Navy Royal became the Royal Navy, transitioning from a semi-privatized body into a state-controlled entity. With the change came a new career-driven officer corps. With officers came privilege and a distinct alcohol-based class structure aboard ship. The seamen drank rum; the officers were entitled to gin.

As far back as the 1700s, quartermasters supervised the provisioning of their individual ships; there was minimal, if any, central supervisory authority. As such, the ships often stocked the gin of their local port. Bristol and Liverpool, both naval hubs, had their own styles of gin, but these are now lost. In London, the Gordon & Co. distillery, founded in 1769 by Alexander Gordon, quickly made a name for itself with both the British and merchant navies, whose men spread Gordon's Gin to the four corners of the world.

By 1850, Plymouth Gin – produced outside of London in the coastal city of Plymouth – was supplying the Royal Navy with upwards of 1,000 barrels a year of custom-made 100 UK proof gin (57 per cent ABV/114 US proof). The concept of this gutsy 'Naval Strength' gin evolved for good reason. Alcohol and gunpowder were originally stored together under lock and key to avoid the potential for the crew getting drunk and having easy access to firearms. This dual storage, however, posed a serious risk: if standard-proof alcohol leaked on the gunpowder, the powder would fail to ignite. The industrious creation of a 100 proof gin allowed for spillage on the powder without deleterious effects because it contained more alcohol than water.

One of gin's beneficial traits was that it covered up the unpleasant taste of various medicinal treatments. Angostura bitters was created in 1824 by Dr J. G. Siegert as 'a useful remedy in all complaints arising from Weakness and Sluggishness of the Digestive Organs, Malaria, Colic, Diarrhoea and Colds'. For the Navy's purposes, however, it was a cure for seasickness. Gin and bitters evolved as a way to disguise the acrid taste of the herbal tonic.

Called 'Gin Pahit', meaning 'bitter', in British Malaysia, gin and bitters soon earned the whimsical label 'Pink Gin', because of the pinkish-brown hue left by the bitters. This was the name embraced by authors from Somerset Maugham to Graham Greene, who held the drink as a symbol of British colonialism. By the late nineteenth century, Pink Gin had made its way back to London and had begun to appear in bars and clubs. Today, 'pinkers', as it is sometimes affectionately known, is still a quintessentially British drink.

Another serious shipboard concern was scurvy, caused by the lack of vitamin C in the sailors' diet. Beginning in 1614, John Woodall, Surgeon General of the British East India Company, recommended lemons, limes and oranges for their antiscorbutic effects. Not surprisingly, when citrus was issued as part of the seamen's rations – a notable example being the crew sailing under Admiral Edward Vernon, which enjoyed its daily 'tot' of grog (rum cut with water, plus citrus to compensate for the foulness of the water) – no serious symptoms of scurvy presented themselves.

While many other antiscorbutic agents, namely vinegar and low-salt diets, were also popular at the time, the continuing success of citrus to fight and prevent scurvy led naval surgeon James Lind, in 1747, to conduct the world's first clinical trial to ascertain – and confirm – the effectiveness of said fruits. By 1795, the Admiralty had accepted medical recommendations that lemon juice be issued to the fleet. Eventually, limes replaced lemons since they grew plentifully in the British West Indies and because Britain was often at war with those countries that produced lemons. The prevalent use of limes in the Navy is what earned British sailors the epithet 'Limeys'.

All this is preamble to the Gimlet, a very proper and classic gin drink made solely of the juniper spirit and a sort of sweetened lime juice syrup generally known as a cordial, usually one specific brand: Rose's Lime Cordial. In all likelihood, Navy men had already thought to combine their lime ration and their gin, but the resulting drink was in no way a

Advertisement for Gilbey's Gin, 'The International Gin', 1935. Note the references in imagery and text to the concept of Empire.

A collection of mostly pre-Prohibition Plymouth Gin bottles, *c.* 1900–1910. The blue capped bottle is from the 1970s. It was said that when the monk's feet got dry it was time for a new bottle. The logo was changed in 2006.

true classic Gimlet, whose pungent flavour is unique in the cocktail kingdom. One could argue that without Rose's there would most likely have been no Gimlet at all.

Patented by Lauchlin Rose in 1867, the lightly sweetened, non-alcoholic preserved lime juice mixer appealed to the cost-effectiveness of naval minds, not to mention their palates; it also managed to carve out a place in the civilian market, which was in the early throes of Temperance. Prior to this, citrus had been preserved – to varying degrees of effectiveness – through boiling, the addition of alcohol, or with chemicals such as tartaric acid. In 1850, *Miss Leslie's Lady's New Receipt-Book* employs cream of tartar 'to preserve lemon juice for a voyage'; the book also notes that only the best and freshest lemons must be used as 'one that is in the least bit tainted will spoil the whole.' Rose's cordial was not only a safely produced juice product, but it avoided the mandated 15 per cent alcohol as preservative.

Many theories exist as to how lime cordial made its way to naval and merchant vessels; cocktail historian David Wondrich suggests that it might have appealed to the officers because of its apparent health benefits and as a mark of luxury to distinguish themselves from the sailors. We do know that as far back as Lind, naval lime juice rations were administered with an equal dose of sugar, setting the template for the commercial products, such as Rose's, which would spring up to meet the increased demand for quality lime juice provided for in the Merchant Shipping Act of 1867.

While arguments abound, the British Royal Navy attributes the Gimlet's name to naval Surgeon General Sir Thomas D. Gimlette, who served from 1879 to 1913. The Navy's *Covey Crump*, a dictionary of slang terms, lists a 'Gimlette' as a drink of 'gin laced with lime cordial', which was introduced by the good doctor in hopes of encouraging his fellow officers to drink their lime juice. It is worth noting, however, that there was no mention of the famed drink in the doctor's 1943 obituary, or specification that Rose's be the cordial. Other sources more esoterically suggest that the gimlet, a sharp, pointed corkscrew used to open casks of spirits aboard ship, gave the drink its moniker.

In any case, the Gimlet is mentioned by name in *The Admiral: The Memoirs of Albert Gleaves, USN* wherein the author, travelling in China in 1920, tells us, 'At a club I was given a new drink called a gimlet – a mild affair of gin, lime juice and water.' As a recipe, the Gimlet appears in print in Harry MacElhone's 1927 cocktail book *Barflies and Cocktails*. The recipe calls for a one-to-one ratio of Coates Plymouth Gin and Rose's Lime Cordial, noting that the mixture is 'a very popular beverage in the Navy'. Over the years, the proportions have been toyed with to varying degrees and other ingredients have worked their way into the recipe. In his *Jigger, Beaker, and Glass* (1939), Charles H. Baker Jr suggests cutting the pungency of the lime cordial with a teaspoon of gomme syrup or sugar, which produces a smoother drink. Today, the vodka gimlet is the more likely version, thus necessitating that one specifically request a gin gimlet. Regardless, countless devotees of Rose's funky, sweet-sour flavour insist that the only true Gimlet is made from Rose's and gin.

The Navy continued to use gin as a creative way to 'take its medicine' and a drinking culture grew up around it. When ships docked, they ran up a green and white flag that signalled an open invitation to 'come aboard and share a drink' for officers in that port. The 'gin pennant', as it is known, still exists today.

Like the Royal Navy, the soldiers of the British East India Company found industrious uses for gin. Whereas scurvy was the killer aboard ship, malaria was a deadly threat on land. Quinine, derived from the bark of the Cinchona tree, became the accepted, but unsavoury, medicine. To ease the daily treatments, the soldiers took to dosing their quinine with water, sugar and lime. Gin was added a bit later. If this sounds familiar, it is; this is the precursor to the archetypal British gin drink, the gin and tonic.

By 1858, 'Indian tonic water' (courtesy of Erasmus Bond) had appeared on the market, simplifying preparation. In 1870, the Schweppes Company introduced their own version of tonic water, which is considered by many to be indispensible to today's G&T. Whether drinking a gin and tonic, Pink Gin or a Gimlet, British colonials took the practical and made it pleasurable. Later, as expatriates trickled back from India and elsewhere, they brought their taste for these drinks with them.

Gin Palaces

As the British Empire was redrawing the world map, the Industrial Revolution was changing the entire appearance and structure of Britain, and of London in particular. This newly industrialized society brought with it both problems and rewards. The creation of factories lured workers to the cities once again and, consequently, London's population boomed. Peter Cunningham's *Hand-book of London* (1850) showed an increase from 864,854 persons in 1801 to 1,870,127 persons in 1841. With the continued growth of the city came issues of general welfare. Cholera epidemics in 1831 and 1848 led to a revolution in hygiene; the era of free trade made food more available and less costly. Poverty had not been eradicated, but it was being confronted for the first time in England's history. Meanwhile, a powerful working class had emerged and was challenging the old ways of thinking. All in all, a vast reshuffling of the existing social order was afoot.

Further, advances in every area of technology began to reshape the urban landscape. Machine tools made the cost-effective manufacture of decorative furnishings a possibility. In 1807, Frederick Albert Winsor illuminated Pall Mall with gas lamps, replacing the dim oil lamps of the 1700s. Meanwhile, mainland Europe had invented a new process for making glass, making its use more accessible for everyday buildings; in 1832, the Chance brothers created sheet glass, which allowed for large panes of glass to be fitted together.

All these innovations set the stage for the sensorial delight of the gin palace, which became a home away from home for the lower classes. In 1836, Charles Dickens offered a rather unbiased description of these festive gathering places in *Sketches by Boz*, which chronicled the everyday world of London Town:

Thomas Rowlandson, *Rum Characters in a Shrubbery*, 1808, hand-coloured etching. An example of a pre-Gin Palace gin shop. 'Booth's Best Gin' is stencilled on the left barrel.

All is light and brilliancy . . . the gay building with the fantastically ornamented parapet, the illuminated clock, the plate-glass windows surrounded by stucco rosettes, and its profusion of gas-lights in richly-gilt burners, is perfectly dazzling when contrasted with the darkness and dirt we have just left. The interior is even gayer than the exterior. A bar of French-polished mahogany, elegantly carved, extends the whole width of the place; and there are two side-aisles of great casks, painted green and gold, enclosed within a light brass rail.

The first of these splendid fixtures was most likely Thompson and Fearon's on Holborn Hill, established in late 1829 or early 1830. Designed by the architect John B. Papworth, Fearon's established the future layout of the palace with its long counter, lack of seating and open room; all of these elements were incorporated with the specific idea of briskly moving business in and out. More importantly, as noted in Peter Haydon's *An Inebriated History of Britain* (2005), the traditional roles of welcoming host and weary traveller had transformed into a business relationship motivated by a simple exchange of goods.

Ironically, the Beer Act of 1830, which was meant to slow the spread of what would become a new sort of gin fever, achieved the opposite, encouraging the growth of the gin palace. England existed under a 'tied' system in which the pub owner had to purchase his beer from a specific brewer. The Beer Act dissolved this pseudo-monopoly and allowed anyone to sell beer with the purchase of a cheap licence. Over a period of eight years, 45,000 beer shops appeared across the country. The gin distillers had no choice but to fight back with something just as seductive as plentiful beer.

As Dickens noted, the palaces were seduction personified. With alluring names like 'The Cream of the Valley', 'The Out and Out' and 'The No Mistake', it was difficult to resist the charm of one's local watering-hole. The surface glamour and conviviality of the gin palace actually did a good deal to elevate gin's image, slowly establishing the idea that drinking was a social sport, not just a means to oblivion.

From Old Tom to London Dry

During the Gin Craze, alcohol was more of a delivery system for intoxication than a drink to be savoured. All that changed at the dawn of the nineteenth century. It is not hyperbole to say that the Industrial Revolution affected every aspect of life and certainly everything to do with gin production.

In the wake of the Craze, lacklustre harvests from 1757 to 1760 led Britain to declare a prohibition on distilling grain. This naturally led to a decrease in gin consumption – and a far healthier populace – for a brief period. Then, in 1760, the ban on distilling was lifted and gin was once again the darling of the people, although it was not quite so deadly thanks to new regulations. By raising excise duties and instituting stringent quality controls, Parliament hoped to ensure that gin was no

An etching of a typical gin palace, late 19th century. Note the 'Old Tom' beside the 'Cream of the Valley' barrel.

longer the killer spirit it had been; the bottom line was that the gin cost more to make, so the quality had to improve to justify the price.

Bradstreet's 'Old Tom' had become a generalized name for gin. It was sold in barrels to retailers, who often sweetened it themselves and served it neat like a cordial. During the Craze, the added sugar was intended to disguise the foul flavours of poor-quality alcohol; as gin entered the nineteenth century, it was sweetened to cater to the prevailing tastes.

Thus begins a rather shadowy period of gin's development, with the old styles slowly giving way to the styles we know today. During the Craze, spirits were made by anyone who could gain access to ingredients and a still; the result, as

Generic label 'Old Tom' gin bottle, *c.* 1870s. A lovely example featuring the original 'cat-and-barrel' symbol.

The Tanqueray Gin distillery on Goswell Road, London, 1911.

we have seen, was always noxious and often deadly. In the era of the gin palace, gin gradually became more drinkable thanks to new production techniques and an influential class of professional distillers – Alexander Gordon, Felix Booth, Charles Tanqueray, James Burroughs, and Walter and Alfred Gilbey.

Driven by ambition and emboldened by the Industrial Age, these men sought to make quality products, and their companies originally produced a variety of styles. For example, early recipe books from Alexander Gordon show that he was making a large range of cordial gins in the 1800s; along with sloe (the fruit of the blackthorn tree), damson, blackcurrant and even citrus flavours, the company was also producing an Old Tom gin.

Regardless of how pure their ingredients were, the distillers faced a major hurdle in production. Because they used old-school pot stills, the gin had to be made in small, time-consuming batches. All that changed in 1830. To be perfectly accurate, we should say 1827, for this is when Robert Stein invented the continuous still. In 1830, an enterprising Irish excise officer named Aeneas Coffey discovered Stein's invention and patented it under his own name after making a few modifications.

Unlike the alembic, or pot still, the Coffey Still, which is similar to the one invented by Cellier Blumenthal, has some distinct advantages. A continuous still, as the name suggests, can distill alcohol without interruption. Moreover, it produces a 'clean' spirit without any impurities and a higher concentration of alcohol in the final distillation. Therefore a distiller does not need to add 'ingredients' like oil of turpentine and sulphuric acid, nor is sugar necessary (although at the time it was still desired) to cover up foul flavours.

Old Tom's popularity grew exponentially after the invention of the Coffey still, which allowed for a more delicate balance between sugar and botanicals. It became, to all intents and purposes, a nascent dry gin that was sweetened. Whereas Old Tom had started life as more of a malty, pot-still gin, it was evolving into a cleaner, more herbal one. For this reason, the Old Tom style is frequently called the 'missing link' between Dutch genever with its whisky-like undertones and London Dry gin with its dependence on botanicals.

In considering how these gins – whether Old Tom or London Dry – were made, it is essential to forget what we know of modern production techniques. In *The New Mixing Book* (1869), geared primarily to the spirits seller, we get a glimpse into the machinations of the business. Even at this late date, gin was sold to publicans by the barrel and the pub owner then sold it by the glass or bottled it for his customers to take away.

At the time, gin could be purchased sweetened or unsweetened from the distiller. Apparently, there was some concern that a pre-sweetened gin might cheat the publican of product because the book offers measurements for sugaring the gin in the pub and advises that 'the taste of each locality of class of customers must, of course, govern the amount of sweetening.' The author also gives us a glimpse into the palate of various social classes when he claims that 'strong or unsweetened gin is in comparatively little request and then with few exceptions only amongst the respectable or monied classes.'

This 'strong or unsweetened gin' refers to the then-emerging London Dry style. The term 'dry', specifically chosen to denote unsweetened gin, was coined to differentiate it from sugared products. As noted, the wealthier classes took a liking to this drier style, but it received further validation during the Victorian era when an emphasis on healthy living took hold. In keeping with the trend, gin distillers started to advertise their gin as 'sugar-free' or 'dry'. The gimmick worked; Old Tom, with its sweet profile, simply did not fit the new lifestyle and, although it continued to be made until the 1960s by many companies, its glory days were over.

What the Coffey Still did beautifully was to clear the way for the development of the bright, clean, pure style that is associated with London Dry gin. Moreover, it made large-scale mass production a reality, allowing the great gin brands to be born. And without the competition of sugar or other flavourings, the now-familiar botanicals – juniper, as well as the bright lemony character of coriander, and the slight woodiness of angelica, among others – could take centre stage, becoming the hallmarks of this now-classic style.

The oldest dedicated gin distillery in England appears to be G&J Greenall's. Records indicate that the original owner, Thomas Dakin, began distilling in 1761, almost immediately after the ban on using grain for spirits was lifted. Dakin's gin quickly got a reputation for being far more refined than the rough product being served in London. Other distillers soon followed, as seen in the timeline below:

1769 – Alexander Gordon opens the Gordon & Co. distillery in London's Southwark area. In 1786 the distillery is relocated to Clerkenwell due to the purity of the water from the natural spring at the Clerk's Well.

1778 – Booth's and its sister company Boord's are listed in the Directory of Merchants.

Gordon's Special Dry London Gin bottle, 1909–23.

Booth's Distillery in Cowcross Street, Smithfield, *c.* 1820. Booth's, one of the original London Dry gin producers, is still available today.

1830 – Charles Tanqueray launches Tanqueray & Co. By 1895 records show he is shipping gin to America.

1863 – James Burrough founds Beefeater.

1867 – Walter and Alfred Gilbey move from the wine business to the spirits business, starting Gilbey's Gin.

1898 – Tanqueray merges with Gordon & Co., taking over their current Goswell Road site.

Over what amounts to roughly a century, the hierarchy of London Dry gin was established. From 1820 to 1840, the existing distillers formed the Rectifier's Club, a rather incestuous group whose purpose was to protect each other's interests – be it through price-fixing, quality control or intermarriage.

Unlike the questionable gin of the prior century, the gins of Gordon's, Tanqueray and the like were quality products, whose makers sourced exotic botanicals and ran their spirit through multiple steps of purification.

Still dry but considered by many to be more aromatic, Plymouth Gin is separate and distinct from the London Dry style. According to the Plymouth timeline, theirs was the first real 'dry' gin, albeit not London Dry, since it was produced outside the confines of that city. In 1793, the Coates family opened their gin distillery in the Black Friars Monastery, which had been a malt house since 1697. In the 1730s, the first reference to 'the strength of the Plymouth water' was made; it is most likely that this gin was in the sweetened style of Old Tom.

Plymouth was a much sought-after brand, particularly by the Royal Navy, whose officers considered it the only choice for a proper Pink Gin. Because it was so often imitated, the distillery engaged in numerous lawsuits to protect the name. Today, Plymouth has European Union protected status, allowing only gin produced within the ancient city walls to be labelled as Plymouth Gin. Along with their London cousins, distillers in Plymouth set the stage for gin's modern evolution.

Gin Becomes Respectable

As regulation increased and production techniques evolved, gin's quality and reputation improved markedly. In 1850, Felix Booth, of Booth's Gin, convinced Parliament to lift a ban on gin exports. Soon after, English gin made its way round the world; there are even records in old Gordon's company ledgers of a delivery to Australia with payment being made in gold dust. The term 'English gin' quickly became a hallmark of a quality product.

During this time, the growing middle classes began to embrace gin in a number of ways. According to cocktail historian David Wondrich:

> Gin punch . . . was the drink that made gin-drinking acceptable for the middle class. From its origins in the 1730s as, essentially, an underclass parody of what the rich folks were doing, it became a staple of summer tippling for the flannels-and-croquet set.

From roughly the 1840s to the 1880s, punches became elaborate presentations, accented by fresh ingredients. It was the era of *Cooling Cups and Dainty Drinks*, as William Terrington's 1869 recipe book was titled. Along with various punches, the book featured the Gin Cocktail, proving that the Cocktail – created in America – had reached England by this time. Terrington described the drink by saying, 'Cocktails are compounds very much used by "early birds" to fortify the inner man.'

Another mainstay of the more privileged class was the Pimm's No. 1 brand, created in 1823. James Pimm's Oyster Bar was one of London's most popular spots, where the 'dandiest city gents' indulged in oysters and gin. The gin was still a little rough around the edges at this time, leading the customers to gulp rather than relish it. The enterprising Pimm created the 'house cup', as it was first known, taking gin as a base and blending herbs, spices and liqueurs into it. This house cup gave way to a plethora of what are now known as 'fruit cups' or 'summer cups', defined as a spirit- or wine-based drink flavoured with herbs and spices and topped with lemonade or some other fizzy mixer; Plymouth, among others, produces one.

Pimm's No. 1 liqueur was exported as far as Colombo, Sri Lanka, where it was served at the posh Galle Face Hotel, and

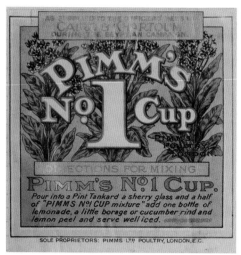

An early bottle label for the Pimm's No. 1 Cup brand.

to the Sudan, where it was drunk by Sir Horatio Kitchener's officers during the 1898 campaign. The traditional way to drink a fruit cup is as a 'long' drink in a tall glass mixed with lemonade, ginger ale or the like and garnished with an assortment of sliced fruits, including apples, strawberries, lemon and orange, as well as mint and cucumber. It is the epitome of summertime leisure.

In addition to its presence in Pimm's liqueur and sloe or damson liqueurs, gin as an ingredient debuted in *Mrs Beeton's Book of Household Management* (1861). The book sold over a million copies in its first weeks, and Beeton herself garnered the status of a Victorian Martha Stewart. In the same year, gin became available at retail shops and gin cordials began popping up at proper Victorian ladies' tea parties. The ladies called it 'white wine' or labelled the bottle 'nig' – gin spelled backwards – to confuse the servants.

Around the same time, gentlemen of breeding started to drink gin in their clubs; the 1871 recipe book entitled *The*

Gentleman's Table Guide catered to the social desire to serve drinks and entertain in one's home. Among the drinks featured were the Gin Twist, the Gin Julep and the Gin Sangaree.

Giving gin an even greater advantage was the 1863 phylloxera epidemic, which destroyed almost all the vineyards in Europe. Ironically, the blight was caused by English botanists who brought infected samples of vines back from America. Britain's vineyards were all wiped out, but no one cared about British wine. It was the loss of France's grapes that indirectly caused a spike in gin consumption as British high society looked for a substitute for their usual cognac.

Still, as the popularity and general respectability of gin grew, the very public and boisterous locales of the gin palaces

Plymouth Gin still house, 1906.

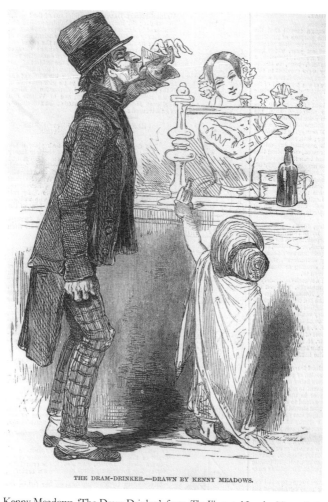

THE DRAM-DRINKER.—DRAWN BY KENNY MEADOWS.

Kenny Meadows, 'The Dram Drinker', from *The Illustrated London News*, 1848.

– there were often two or more on the high streets of the city of London – concerned the middle and upper classes. As had happened during the Craze, gin continued to lure women and children into its dens of iniquity. A sketch by caricaturist

Kenny Meadows entitled 'The Dram Drinker' ran in the *Illustrated London News* on 6 May 1848. In the picture, a tattered gent gulps a shot of gin while a small child gamely hands an empty bottle up to the barman. The sketch ran with this commentary:

> Women and children even are coming in with bottles; some of the latter so little, that, like the one which our artist has so truthfully sketched, they are scarcely able to reach up and place the bottle upon the zinc-covered bar . . . Even these young miserable creatures are fond of drink, and may sometimes be seen slyly drawing the cork outside the door, and lifting the poisonous potion to their white withered lips. They have already found that gin numbs and destroys for a time the gnawing pangs of hunger, and they can drink the fiery mixture in its raw state.

Such language galvanized those who opposed the trend toward conspicuous consumption. And so, with alcohol came reformers.

Gin and the Temperance Movement

The nineteenth-century Temperance Movement was instigated by middle class do-gooders who found the public drunkenness displayed by the lower classes distasteful. Fuelled by the moral zeal of philanthropists and the clergy, these people took a 'short pledge' of abstinence, eschewing hard liquor like gin, but not wine and its cousins. Teetotalism, the bastion of the working class, arose as a reaction to the hypocrisy of Temperance activists, who sought to tell the lower classes to avoid drinking gin while finding middle-class tipples such as wine perfectly acceptable. Those preaching teetotalism were almost evangelical in their hatred of drink.

Among the loudest of the individual critics was Charles Dickens's illustrator George Cruikshank, a man quite famous in his own right. Cruikshank was not always an advocate for abstinence; he had a healthy appetite for alcohol until 1842 when he suddenly decided to stop drinking. Even before, however, gin had had a presence in his work, presaging his fanatical teetotalism.

Published in 1835, Cruikshank's vivid etching of *The Gin Juggarnath* depicts an enormous gin palace on wheels crushing the unfortunates trapped beneath it. In the distance, one can see the English countryside, unsullied by gin's wrath. Cruikshank's series entitled *The Bottle* (1847) and *The Drunkard's Children* (1848) vividly decry alcohol as well. In the former, the eight plates chronicle the story of an alcoholic man who

George Cruikshank, *The Gin Juggarnath; or, the Worship of the Great Spirit of the Age!!*, c. 1835, serial etching with hand colour. Its progress is marked by desolation, misery and crime.

George Cruikshank, 'The Gin-crazed Girl Commits Suicide', from the series *The Drunkard's Children*, c. 1848.

murders his wife and is committed to an asylum. In the latter, the story continues, focusing on the man's children, including his daughter, who is seen flinging herself off a bridge. The caption reads in part: 'The poor girl, homeless, friendless, deserted, destitute, and gin mad, commits self-murder.'

Cruikshank's attitudes cost him his friendship with Dickens, who held more moderate beliefs. In contrast to Cruikshank's extremist views, Dickens suggested that:

> Gin-drinking is a great vice in England, but wretchedness and dirt are greater; and until you improve the homes of the poor, or persuade a half-famished wretch not to seek relief in the temporary oblivion of his own misery . . . gin-shops will increase in number and splendour.

Dickens's claims were prescient. The 'gin-shops', as he called them, did indeed flourish. While England started exporting its gin in 1850, gin consumption at home continued to grow, so much so that it garnered concern from one intimately connected to the spirit.

In 1869, Walter Gilbey, whose gin was one of the many great success stories of the era, observed:

> It is the misfortune of this country . . . that strong drinks, chiefly it may be believed from want of knowledge, are as a rule consumed at greater strengths then is necessary either to give pleasure or satisfy thirst.

Gilbey's comment is at once insightful and lacking awareness. While the English had always valued both the strength and amount of their alcohol, the consumption of gin by the lower classes in both the eighteenth and nineteenth centuries was not fuelled by 'want of knowledge'. Rather, it was born of the simple desire to escape from the struggles of everyday life. The 1800s saw vast improvements for the poor and the working class, but there was still much to accomplish. In the meantime, the gin palace gave comfort in the storm.

Despite this fact, the stand on abstinence continued to be put forward by both Temperance societies and members of the government. In 1892, a bill instigated by Dr Jayne, the bishop of Chester, was placed before Parliament. Jayne suggested a model for Temperance based on the successful Swedish Gothenburg system, which increased state control and discouraged the sale of liquor. If the system were put into play, Jayne said, 'the mere drink shop, the gin palace, and "the bar" – that pernicious incentive for drinking for drinking's sake – would be utterly abolished.' The bill did not pass, perhaps because many people agreed with the opinion of one unnamed bishop in the House of Lords who said he would 'prefer to see all England free than England sober'.

5
Gin in America

One Martini is all right.
Two is too many.
Three is not enough.
James Thurber

When the Frenchman Alexis de Tocqueville came to America
in 1831 to study democracy in action, he noted:

> The old principles which had governed the world for
> ages were no more; a path without a turn and a field
> without an horizon were opened to the exploring and
> ardent curiosity of man . . . Men are there seen more
> equal in their strength, than in any other country of the
> world, or in any age of which history has preserved the
> remembrance.

What Tocqueville captured in such eloquent prose is the
notion of freedom that has always been the guiding factor in
the American way of life. From the outset, the New World
glowed with untapped promise, and this blank slate attract-
ed colonists who were, by turns, adventurers, dreamers and
entrepreneurs. These rugged individuals faced an untamed

land which lacked any sort of creature comforts – and they bent it to their will. Indeed, the people who would eventually fight for and win their independence were a special breed of straightforward free-thinkers who dreamed big and possessed a 'can-do' spirit.

This sense of – and demand for – freedom worked its way into everything Americans did. Unlike other countries where there is one liquor that tends to define the national identity, such as whiskey in Ireland and whisky in Scotland, tequila in Mexico or genever in the Netherlands, Americans drank freely of whatever tipple they chose, and they did so without the antiquated class constraints they had left behind. Rum, brandy, whiskey and gin – first genever, then English – shared equal shelf space. Freedom to invent without constraints inspired the creation of the cocktail, that quintessentially American beverage.

It is quite possible that alcohol, gin certainly included, played a more vital role in the settlement of America than in any other country. One statistic suggests that in the early nineteenth century, Americans were drinking more than Londoners did during the Gin Craze. What was first used as a fortification – both spiritual and medicinal – in the quest to build a new nation eventually became a panacea for the stress of urbanization and its accompanying effects.

Genever in America

In 1625, the Dutch founded the New Netherlands. In 1640, Willem Kieft, the colony's Director General, founded the first American whiskey distillery on Staten Island; given the era and his nationality, it is likely that Kieft's whiskey used genever-like production techniques but without the juniper.

By 1732, the original thirteen colonies had been established and genever, also known as Hollands, Holland gin and Geneva, could be found in every tavern. Genever possessed enough of a presence by 1741 that a New York crime ring known for stealing genever was dubbed the 'Geneva Club'. Further, records from the Bols archives confirm an incredibly strong trade in the export of Holland gin to America from 1750 to 1800 and, despite a curious lull from 1800 to 1850, again from 1850 to 1916.

It is no coincidence that it was genever – 'a beverage . . . with much the flavor of excellent Hollands' – which American author Washington Irving's slumbering hero in *Rip Van Winkle* (1819) blamed for his twenty-year nap. In fact, in the nineteenth century when cocktail culture was in full swing, roughly five times as much Holland gin was imported as English gin. As late as 1860, John Marquart's *600 Receipts, Worth Their Weight In Gold* offers many recipes for imitating Holland gin, all of which call

Freebooter Geneva bottle, 1895. Despite the influx of London Dry gin, genever still remained popular at the beginning of the 20th century.

Blankenheym & Nolet Hollands Geneva bottle, *c.* 1890s. The English-speaking market eagerly adopted the anglicized term for genever.

for some sort of pure spirit or rectified whiskey and at least a gallon of 'pure imported Holland gin'. In 1883, records indicate that America imported 321,340 imperial gallons (1.46 million litres) of Hollands in bulk, as well as 11,194 cases in bottles. Comparatively, British gin came in at 11,402 gallons in bulk and 7,313 cases. Further, if we look at American distilling guides from earlier in the century, such as *The Practical Distiller* (1809) by Samuel M'Harry, we see that he recommends a distillation process very similar to that used for genever – the use of a pot still, as well as botanicals confined to juniper and perhaps some hops. Until a sweeter style of Old Tom and the more botanical London Dry became commonplace, the gins of America's youth – genever from the Netherlands and early, more malty versions of Old Tom – were clearly rich, bold and most definitely more like whisky than modern English gin.

Mixed Drinks and the Cocktail

In the early years of the Republic, America borrowed the British tradition of the punch bowl, the contents of which were frequently drunk with friends over a few languid hours. The mixed drink was born of this communal punch – spirits, sugar, water, citrus and spice – whose abundance of liquid, as well as the inherent time needed to consume it, did not jibe with the image of industriousness that Americans in this era hoped to present. By the late 1700s, bartenders had taken note and were offering efficient single-serving presentations of punch.

In an almost biblical manner, the bowl of Gin Punch begat a variety of punch-based drinks. The Gin Fix, the Gin Sour, the Gin Daisy and the Gin Fizz were all maddeningly similar but slightly different. What they had in common, however, were elements of the Gin Punch – gin plus sugar, water and citrus. All of these were classified as 'short drinks' – shaken with ice and strained into a small glass. Quick to consume, reasonably priced and infinitely tasty, they offered the average American an easy excuse for a quick tipple during the stressful work day.

Along with the punch, other key mainstays of the drinking culture were the Toddy and the Sling. Toddies, usually drunk hot, and slings, usually drunk cold, were elegant in their simplicity, requiring only spirit, water, sugar and perhaps a bit of nutmeg. They were often prescribed as health-giving tonics, using whatever tipple – genever, whiskey or rum – was preferred.

The Cocktail – not the generic catch-all term for today's mixed drinks, but the specifically named drink of yore – is to all intents a Sling with bitters added. It was born as a convenient, practical way to self-medicate, since doctors were not always easily accessible. Like the British Navy, Americans used bitters as a cure-all. Gold Rushers could make their own from herbs and bark or acquire it from the local snake oil salesman; more civilized folk could purchase it bottled from the corner mercantile. However, ascertaining when this alchemical transformation of adding bitters to spirit first occurred is akin to the chicken and the egg conundrum.

Despite its dodgy birth date, the 'Cocktail' was first defined in printed English on 13 May 1806. The editor of the *Balance and Columbian Repository* newspaper, replying to a query about the use of the word 'Cocktail' in an article, defined it as such: 'Cocktail is a stimulating liquor, composed of *spirits* of any kind, *sugar, water*, and *bitters*. It is vulgarly called *bittered sling*.'

In its youth, the Cocktail was considered a 'morning' drink, implying that there was something to overcome from the night before. As such, it acquired a somewhat unsavoury reputation and was considered the domain of the risqué sporting set. Referring to gamblers, hustlers and the loose women they courted, this term was less complimentary than it might sound. Of course, as with everything new, the Cocktail soon found a home among more 'respectable' folks, who simply could not overlook the fact that the drink was infinitely satisfying. The Cocktail's transition from curative elixir to purposeful refreshment was, as William Grimes points out in *Straight Up or On the Rocks* (1993), 'a turning point' in the way Americans drank.

Both the Cocktail and mixed drinks like the Sour and the Fix were available in the saloons of the day. Whether the grand bar rooms found in the best hotels or the archetypal swinging door establishments of the Old West, saloons offered the atmosphere of a private club – a sort of cultural gathering place – but remained egalitarian. The most elegant of them often resembled the opulently decorated gin palaces of

Postcard depicting 'The Famous H. C. Ramos Gin Fizz Saloon', New Orleans, early 1900s.

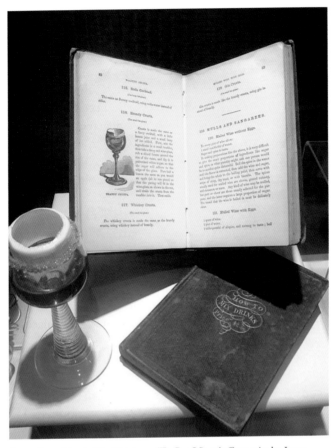

Pages from *How to Mix Drinks; or, The Bon Vivant's Companion* by Jerry Thomas (1862). It was the first cocktail book published.

London. The difference between the American saloon and the gin palace, however, was profound. Gin palaces were designed to lure customers in and then send them quickly on their way. The saloon dazzled its clientele with a fantastical array of drinks served up by nattily dressed bartenders who performed a ballet with shaker and glass.

The most famous of these bartenders-cum-showmen was arguably Jerry Thomas, who is often credited with bringing cocktail culture to Europe and Britain. In 1862 Thomas changed the drink world forever with the publication of *How to Mix Drinks, or the Bon Vivant's Companion*, the first book of its kind. Along with various mixed drinks, the first edition featured ten official cocktails by definition, including the Gin Cocktail, which notably used Holland gin.

In the early years of American mixology, the only gin used was in fact genever. However, in 1850, Great Britain finally started exporting its gins to the USA thanks to Felix Booth's petitions to Parliament. As we have seen, at this time English gin manufacturers were mostly producing Old Tom, as well as various cordial gins such as sloe and damson.

By the late 1800s Old Tom, whose sweeter, more botanical profile now offered a less malty base for drinks, was being called for by name in American bar guides. In the 1887 edition of Thomas's book Holland gin still featured strongly, but Old Tom was the gin of choice for the Martinez (the forerunner of the Martini), as well as the Silver Fizz and the Pineapple Julep. In addition to the original Gin Cocktail with Hollands, there was a new entry for the Old Tom Gin Cocktail.

In George Kappeler's *Modern American Drinks* (1895) 'Tom gin' was called for in numerous cocktails, including the Dundorado, the Ford, the George, the Princeton, the Turf, the Union, the Yale and the York; Holland gin featured only in the Smith, Schiedam and Holland gin cocktails. Holland gin is again mentioned for the John Collins, a 'long drink' composed of gin, sugar, lemon and soda water, served over ice in a tall glass. Tellingly, there is also a Tom Collins, featuring, logically, Tom gin.

In 1872, when Fleischmann's Distillery, the first American dry gin producer, opened in Ohio, the public taste still ran

Fleischmann's Gin advertisement, *c.* 1930s. Fleischmann's was the first American gin, and is still produced today.

toward these sweeter concoctions. Awareness of and an interest in 'dry' was still peripheral at best. Even as late as 1891, *The Flowing Bowl* cocktail book defined 'gin' as 'a very strong liquor manufactured in Holland (Holland gin) and England (Old Tom gin)'.

While the Cocktail and other gin-based mixed drinks continued to be fixtures on bar menus into the late 1800s, it was the dry Martini that would soon capture the imagination of a generation. It would also result in London Dry gin replacing both Holland gin and Old Tom, whose flavour profiles would seem passé by the turn of the century. By 1920, however, changing tastes would matter little as Prohibition cast a pall over the entire country and its interest in drink.

The Road to Prohibition

As the twentieth century arrived, America welcomed some true oddities in the world of gin, seemingly capitalizing on the cocktail's medicinal past. Many of these gins were targeted at women for gynaecological problems or as 'pick-me ups'. The instructions suggested that the ladies drink the 'medicine' neat, or diluted equally with milk or water, warm or cold.

One of the ads for Maple Gin, 'the Woman's Friend', featured a Gibson Girl holding aloft a cup of gin. The gin's producer, Buffalo Distilling, went so far as to publish a six-teen-page pamphlet for the 1901 Pan-American Exposition. One of the inside Maple Gin advertisements included a quote from the *Century Dictionary*, stating: 'Pure gin is an important medicament in many diseases, especially those of the urinary organs.' The booklet also contained recreational drink recipes, 'using for a basis that well-known and most healthful of all stimulators, MAPLE GIN'.

Around the same time, the Ullman Company out of Cincinnati offered another remedy, asking, 'Feel tired? All run down?' Their solution: 'Gin Phosphate will tone you up.' Buchu Gin was another popular remedy sold over the counter at drugstores. The Bouvier Specialty Company called theirs 'A Delightful Beverage. An Excellent Tonic'. Friedenwald's

SEE PAGE 14.—DIRECTIONS FOR THE PREPARATION OF A FEW OF THE MOST HEALTHFUL GIN BEVERAGES.

Maple Gin advertisement, 'The Woman's Friend', 1901. This ad is part of a 16-page catalogue for the Pan-American Exposition in Buffalo. Compliments of Buffalo Distilling Co., makers of Maple Gin, the cover purports to be 'of interest to ladies' and contains eight advertisements touting the product's efficacy.

Buchu Gin advertised in the *World Almanac and Encyclopedia* of 1907 and claimed that the combination of ingredients made it 'a most effective cure for all diseases of the Kidneys, Blood, and Urinary Organs, Female Complaints and Irregularities'. Another novel product was Asparagus Gin, made by the Rothenberg Company out of San Francisco and the Folsom Company, among others. Asparagus, like juniper berries, is considered a diuretic, thus its application here.

While medicinal alcohol was not looked at askance, alcohol for pleasure had its detractors. These activists were not without cause. In fact, as noted in *The Prevention and Societal Impact of Drug and Alcohol Abuse* (1999), the decades following the Revolutionary War – a period of stark social and economic

Buchu Gin bottle, recommended 'for all kidney troubles', *c.* 1900. A commercial bottling of a long-time home remedy.

Fag-Co. Asparagus Gin bottle, *c.* 1900s: one of the many 'medicinal' gins that appealed to the public because of its supposed health benefits.

change – saw what is possibly the highest alcohol consumption in America's history. By the early nineteenth century, Americans – primarily men – drank to excess, consuming approximately ten gallons (38 litres) of hard liquor annually. The authors of the above book aptly characterize it: 'Alcohol, which had been the "good creature of God", was becoming "Demon rum".' Temperance groups managed to cut alcohol consumption in the mid-1800s and their cause only gained momentum as the new century dawned.

Driven mainly by women, many of whom had suffered at the hands of drunken men, the anti-alcohol crusade gained momentum during the First World War. It was no small coincidence that groups like the Women's Christian Temperance Union and the Anti-Saloon League flooded Congress with their pleas for abstinence when much of America's male populace was off fighting the war. On 16 January 1919, the politicians bowed to the apparent 'will of the people' and ratified the Eighteenth Amendment, also known as the Volstead Act. (A year later, not coincidentally, women were granted the right to vote.)

The 'will of the people' was anything but. Lyrics from 'The Alcoholic Blues', written in 1919, soon after Prohibition was announced, lament, 'So long high-ball, so long gin. Oh, tell me when you comin' back agin?' This sense of loss echoed across the country. Despite obvious differences in scope and outcome, Prohibition was, in many ways, the American version of the Gin Craze. Like the Gin Acts in the 1700s, the Volstead Act attempted to outlaw alcohol production and sales, but simply drove both underground, often with deadly consequences.

On 16 January 1920, one year to the day after the law had been passed, the Volstead Act was put into action. The United States was officially 'dry'. The spectre of Prohibition sought to take away the pleasure and comfort that alcohol offered without apology. Overnight, saloons were shuttered and all alcohol in stores and bars was confiscated. Almost immediately, a counterculture sprang up as enterprising Americans found creative ways to keep the liquor flowing.

The nineteenth-century legal saloon very quickly became the twentieth-century illegal speakeasy. In New York alone there were 30,000 illegal clubs, including the Cotton Club, the Stork Club and the 21 Club, known for having the best-quality liquor available for its posh clientele. Walter Winchell, then a gossip columnist at the *Daily Mirror*, introduced the term 'gintellectuals' to describe the New York cocktail crowd.

Leaving behind the propriety of Victoriana, the Roaring Twenties were exactly what the name suggested. They were brassy, sexy and rather out of control. Speakeasies, which

Will Carleton, 'The Serpent of the Still', from *City Legends* (1898), engraving.

popped up in numbers comparable to those of the dram shops of eighteenth-century London, were accessed with special passwords. Once inside, one was bombarded by the freely flowing alcohol, the new sound of jazz and the allure of the reckless, wild flapper.

The flapper, who replaced the demure Gibson Girl of yore, was often seen arm in arm with a local gangster, who controlled the liquor supply. Among these gangsters was Al Capone, who was a little-known crook before Prohibition. Capone was king of both liquor and the speakeasies, roughly 10,000 of them, in Chicago. Powerful and brutal, he was emblematic of Prohibition's rampant crime wave, which was engendered by competitive liquor production and aided by government corruption.

British gin companies did not stop doing business simply because Congress decreed that America should stop drinking. The Distillers Company Limited, which owned Gordon's and Tanqueray among others, had an entire series of procedures for covertly delivering their products to the States. While the DCL ostensibly shipped their spirits to Canada, Gilbey's sent their gin to Antwerp and Hamburg first. The shipments were

Gordon & Co.'s Dry Gin 'export' bottle, 1908–20. Produced under licence from the English Gordon's Company in the US.

then sent just outside the international limit of US waters and smuggled into the States by whatever boats could carry them.

Bootlegged liquor also became commonplace, and gin was the easiest spirit to replicate. Whiskey required ageing, something opportunistic moonshiners could ill afford. An ambitious 'distiller' could produce a basic product simply by blending raw alcohol with juniper extract in a large container. Bathtubs were the perfect size for mixing, thus the euphemistic term 'bathtub gin'. It was so easy to make that even the author William Faulkner was known to brew up a batch for himself and his friends, using Cuban alcohol and flavouring it with juniper essence, which could be purchased at a local shop.

While home distillers like Faulkner exercised more control over their spirits, the gin made by moonshiners and sold by bootleggers was far less reputable. Mimicking the gin of the Craze, this base spirit was adulterated and unpalatable. In order to discourage the use of industrial alcohol for liquor production, the government ordered it denatured with toxic methyl alcohol, despite the medical community's objections.

Regardless of the danger, many people 'acquired' industrial alcohol to make their own home brews. Toward the end of Prohibition, various companies capitalized on this 'hobby', advertising synthetic flavourings that mimicked the taste of various spirits including rye, gin and rum. In a 1932 issue of the *New Yorker*, the Pichel Company claimed that 'A jar of PEEKO makes a gallon (Gin type makes TWO) and only 75 cents at your nearest Food or Drug Store.' As an added bonus, the ad claimed, 'The mixing's easy and requires NO AGING!' While products like Peeko were not a danger, the seduction they offered people to make their own ersatz spirits was a problem. By the end of Prohibition, roughly 10,000 people had died from consuming denatured alcohol, its flavour disguised in 'cocktails' dosed with fruit juice and any other mixer available.

'Four in One'
gin flavouring,
c. 1930s.

One of the law's many contradictions was the allowance for continued home use of spirits purchased prior to Prohibition. For those who had industriously stockpiled liquor before the Volstead Act's enforcement, conspicuous consumption was the norm. Gin and whiskey were the most popular spirits; dry Martinis and Manhattans were the drinks of choice. Back in 1892, the Heublein Company had produced pre-mixed 'Club Cocktails' for the home entertainer. During Prohibition, these bottled drinks were no longer available, but the fashion for them continued with the 'cocktail party', the first of which was recorded as early as 1917 in St Louis.

This intimate gathering replaced the elaborate Victorian-era dinner party, whose execution required many servants, whose presence was rarely, if ever, seen in middle-class, twentieth-century America. It was far easier for a host to mix up a Martini than it was to supervise a ten-course meal. The cocktail party also did a great deal for women's rights. In *Domesticating Drink: Women, Men, and Alcohol in America, 1870–1940* (2001), author Catherine Gilbert Murdock observes, 'The cocktail provided hard liquor, but softened . . . Women who would never think of consuming straight gin could ask for a dry Martini without fearing for their reputation.'

Despite the availability of alcohol and one's ability to skirt the edges of the law, many Americans who had the means simply left the country. Doing so not only allowed for far easier access to alcohol, but also an excuse to travel and an implied protest over government-mandated social repression.

Sanctuary could be found in a multitude of places. If one pined for the exotic, Cuba was a short trip away. For those looking to globe-trot, the refined Raffles Hotel in Singapore was at one's disposal. There the house drink was the Singapore sling. Invented in 1915, it featured Beefeater Gin mixed with Benedictine, Cointreau, cherry liqueur, pineapple and lime juices, and bitters.

Across the Atlantic, all of Europe was at one's disposal. Many Americans booked passage on the grand ocean liners of the day, particularly Cunard's RMS *Aquitania*. Once in international waters, liquor was there for the asking. Indeed, during the Depression, when travel fell off, Cunard advertised low-cost trips to the Mediterranean, which were dubbed 'Booze Cruises'.

On the Continent, the cocktail tradition was very much alive as Europeans embraced the American mixed drink. In Paris, the most famous haunt was Harry's New York Bar, run by Scotsman Harry MacElhone, who acquired it in 1923 from his American employer. Harry's Bar gave rise to several famous gin-based cocktails, including the Monkey Gland (a combination of dry gin, orange juice, grenadine and absinthe or pastis). Created at the start of Prohibition in 1923, the Monkey Gland was so named because of a notorious surgical procedure wherein a monkey testicle was grafted onto that of a human male to sexually revive him. Testifying to the popularity of the drink – and the surgery – was a 1923 tune by the Memphis Melody Boys with the line, 'It was a monkey gland that made a monkey out of me.'

Among the expatriates who haunted spots like Harry's Bar were Ernest Hemingway and his good friend F. Scott Fitzgerald. While in France and Italy, lifelong alcoholic Fitzgerald wrote his classic indictment of the Roaring Twenties, *The Great Gatsby* (1925). In the book, Gin Rickeys flowed freely and Gatsby himself was exposed as a bootlegger whose 'side-street drugstores' were selling 'grain alcohol over the counter'.

London cocktail culture was in full swing as well. The most popular spot was the American Bar – a general term to announce that American cocktails were served – at the Savoy Hotel. Tended by American bartender Harry Craddock, who fled the US in 1920 because of Prohibition, the bar was a gathering place for the rich, famous and powerful. Among the best known drinks was the Hanky-Panky, created by Craddock's predecessor Ada Coleman. The Hanky-Panky was essentially a sweet Martini in its mix of one-and-a-half ounces each of gin and sweet vermouth. Then Coleman added the secret ingredient – two dashes of Fernet Branca, an Italian bitters-like digestive.

In 1930, Craddock collected the bar's recipes in *The Savoy Cocktail Book*, a true testament to the drinks of the era. One of Craddock's best known recipes was the gin-based 'Corpse Reviver No. 2', of which he advised, 'Four of these taken in quick succession will unrevive the corpse again.' It was one of over 200 Savoy recipes that called for dry gin generically. Additionally, 27 drinks specified Plymouth Gin and several used Beefeater. As a reflection of the changing times, Old Tom was only featured five times; Hollands was used but twice.

Among those who were linked to the Savoy was the great British playwright, songwriter and all-round wit Noël Coward. No stranger to the juniper spirit, Coward celebrated it as the drink of a generation in his 1926 stage play *Words and Music*: 'For Gin in cruel sober truth supplies the fuel for flaming Youth.'

Those who preferred to mix their drinks at home could use 'Ready-to-Serve Shaker Cocktails'. Created in 1924 by Gordon's Gin, they were meant to celebrate the 'Spirit of the Jazz Age' (Jazz Age being a term coined by Fitzgerald). Much like Heublein's versions for the US market, each cocktail – the term now being used as a catch-all – came with its own individual shaker pre-packaged with the ingredients to mix up a 50/50, a Martini, a dry Martini, a Perfect and a Piccadilly. A year later, Plymouth Gin published its first cocktail booklet, featuring classics like the dry Martini, the Gimlet and the Pink Gin. The original Cocktail never did reach the British masses, who preferred their gin simply mixed with tonic, bitters or ginger beer. One of the most popular combinations in pubs was the Dog's Nose, a shot of gin dropped into a pint of ale or porter.

Amid the shadow of Prohibition, the drink culture flourished in the USA and even spread to the UK and Europe, in great part because of Americans' determination to drink, whether they had to break US law or travel abroad, taking their cocktail culture with them. One of the great ironies of Prohibition is that, despite legislation, Americans drank more during Prohibition than they had before it was enacted. A *Time* magazine article written on 4 December 1933, just as Prohibition was being repealed, observed:

In 1913 the US drank 135,000,000 gal. of rye and Bourbon, 5,000,000 gal. of gin, 1,500,000 gal. of Scotch, a trickle of Irish . . . The Prohibition liquor business was an alcohol business and liquor consumption rose to at least 200,000,000 gal. a year.

When the 'Noble Experiment' faded into ignominy on 5 December 1933, real alcohol flooded back onto the market as domestic and imported product became quickly available.

Gin had an advantage over the competition for many reasons. As with bootlegging, gin could be made and shipped without any ageing; whiskey companies had been forced to destroy their stock and needed time to replenish their aged spirits. Recognizing the demand, Gordon's opened its first US distillery in 1934. Gilbey's started distilling in America in 1938 and is still made here. Seagram's from Canada started producing a dry gin in 1939; it still commands the North American market today.

From Celebrity to Has-been

When Franklin Delano Roosevelt signed the 21st Amendment repealing Prohibition, he drolly commented, 'I think now would be a good time for a beer.' In fact FDR was a Martini man, although rumours abound that his Martinis were some of the worst his guests had ever tasted. Nonetheless, the fact that the president of the United States drank Martinis regularly – he even served them to his staff during what was affectionately termed 'The Children's Hour' – did not hurt the Martini's fortunes.

Certainly, the Martini's connection with the juniper spirit makes it an essential part of the American gin equation. But, beyond that, we need to ask – why is the Martini important? It is arguably the most famous cocktail in the world and the most debated. According to newspaper man and commentator H. L. Mencken, it is 'the only American invention as perfect as the sonnet'. And Ernest Hemingway believed that the ability to drink a dry Martini was one of the hallmarks of being a man.

In *Martini, Straight Up* (2003), Rutgers Classics professor Lowell Edmunds cogently observes that the Martini sends a series of specific messages. His codification is as follows: it is a distinctly American drink, urban and urbane, denoting high status. It is a man's drink and the drink of adults, not children. It is inherently optimistic and belongs to the past. It is also rife with ambiguities. The Martini is both civilized and un-civilized. It unifies and separates; it is classic and individual; it is sensitive and tough.

Given Edmunds's astute observations, it is no wonder that Nikita Khrushchev called the Martini 'America's most lethal weapon'. Today a dry Martini can be made with either gin or vodka. However, from before pre-Prohibition to the FDR White House, asking for a Martini unequivocally meant you were drinking gin.

Stories of the Martini's evolution are completely unverifi-able and mostly apocryphal. The English wrongly associated it with the Martini and Henry rifle and the Italians gave credit to the Martini & Rossi Company, makers of sweet and dry vermouth. New Yorkers anointed a bartender named Martini di Arma di Taggia, while the city of Martinez, California claims it was invented there. Many other tales fuel the mythology, but there is no conclusive genesis.

Origins aside, historians do agree that the Martinez laid the groundwork for the Martini. O. H. Byron's *Modern Bartender's Guide* (1884) describes the Martinez as a Manhattan cocktail – which was composed of whiskey, sweet vermouth, bitters and gum syrup – with Old Tom gin substituting for the whiskey and Maraschino liqueur for the gum. At the time, tastes ran to the sweeter, so the original drink was anything but 'dry'.

Neither is the 'Martini Cocktail' in *Cocktail Boothby's American Bar-Tender* (1891) a dry one. The drink calls for Old Tom cordial gin and sweet vermouth, but replaces the Maraschino with two new additions – Angostura bitters and a twist of lemon peel. Kappeler's *Modern American Drinks* keeps the lemon, but calls for orange bitters and suggests adding a Maraschino cherry, 'if desired by customer'.

There is no official date or place recorded for the first dry Martini, nor is there any record of what dry gin was used. In the 1880s, bartender William Mulhall of the famed Hoffman House in New York noted that both sweet and dry Martinis were popular, suggesting that some sort of dry gin was indeed available. According to records from Plymouth Gin, *Stuart's Fancy Drinks and How to Mix Them* (1896) contains the first documented recipe for what would soon become known officially as a dry Martini. It used three ingredients – Plymouth Gin, which was already a known commodity, dry vermouth and orange bitters.

During Prohibition, the Martini continued to be served, albeit often in a somewhat transmogrified state since the main ingredient was 'bathtub gin'. Even so, for those who had the means, real Martinis were still available and flowed freely. Among the drink's champions were the members of New York's Algonquin Round Table, including literary greats Dorothy Parker and Robert Benchley. The Algonquin group, which met primarily during the years of Prohibition, was known for its collective – frequently gin-tinged – wit. Parker, the epitome of the racy 'it' girl, is famous for uttering the provocative 'I like to have a Martini. Two at the very most. Three, I'm under the table. Four, I'm under my host.' Similarly, Benchley is often credited with 'I must get out of these wet clothes and into a dry Martini.'

The Martini and liquor in general stumbled a little during the Second World War as distillers produced mostly industrial alcohol. As the 1950s arrived, Americans exhibited a more upright, uptight persona and their drink choices reflected this. The Martini, a relatively staid choice compared to the flights of fancy from decades past, became emblematic of this sensible generation. In point of fact, the 'three-Martini lunch' was a fixture for businessmen well into the 1970s. Today, it has been immortalized in the television series *Mad Men* where the suave characters are rarely without a cigarette or a cocktail glass.

Purists would most certainly contend that a dry Martini means a gin Martini. However, the introduction of the vodka Martini was on the horizon. Despite being little known, vodka had been made in the USA since the 1930s, when a Russian immigrant bought the name and distilling process from Smirnoff. However, it was drunk by an incredibly small portion of the population, primarily Eastern European immigrants yearning for a taste of home.

In 1952, according to the Distilled Spirits Council of the United States, vodka only commanded a minuscule 1 per cent of sales in the spirits industry. After being bought by Heublein, Smirnoff was aggressive in its marketing, targeting California by introducing the Moscow Mule, a cocktail designed expressly to promote vodka. Composed of vodka, ginger beer and a slice of lime, the Moscow Mule debuted in Los Angeles at the Cock 'n Bull Restaurant. Californians embraced the neutral character of the spirit, which mixed with just about anything added to it. In something of a counter attack, Seagram's introduced its own invented cocktail featuring Seagram's Gin and grapefruit juice. Ironically, the name they gave it – the Seabreeze – is now associated with a vodka-based drink.

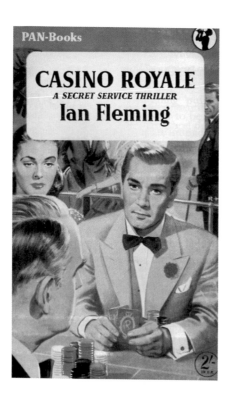

Casino Royale, book jacket, 1955.

In the early 1950s, Smirnoff launched its wildly success-ful 'It leaves you breathless' campaign, highlighting vodka's odourless and flavourless character. The bottom line: it did not leave a trace on the breath – perfect for the three-Martini lunch. In fact, as early as 1951, we find a recipe for a vodka Mar-tini in the cocktail book *Bottom's Up!*, suggesting that it was gaining a presence.

From less than 50,000 cases in 1950, vodka sales reached over one million cases by 1954. In 1955, the quirky term 'vodka-tini' entered the lexicon. And, in the 1960s, when the James Bond films were released, 007 was rarely without his ubiqui-tous 'shaken not stirred' vodka Martini. This was due in no small part to continued shrewd marketing on the part of Smirnoff, which actively wooed the film franchise to feature their vodka instead of gin.

Ironically, when the first Bond book, *Casino Royale*, was published in 1953, Bond drank a concoction of his own making, which featured both gin and vodka, albeit very little of it. The Vesper, as it would be called, combined three parts gin, one part vodka and a half-part of Kina Lillet, which was flavoured with quinine. After his true love Vesper Lynd betrayed him, Bond never drank the Vesper again – nor did it seem to catch the public's fancy. Only recently, thanks to the enthusiasm of cocktail mavens, has the drink been rescued from the ephemera of time.

While Smirnoff taught the public about vodka's merits, James Bond gave vodka an identity – cold, dangerous, seductive – and gin could not compete. Slowly, vodka 'cocktails' started to appear on bar menus. The gin and tonic became the vodka tonic; the Screwdriver and the Bloody Mary dominated. Gin fought back briefly: Gordon's attempted to emphasize its character with ads that reminded customers 'to make sure you have Gordon's in your glass . . . simply ask for Gordon's by name.'

Despite a few minor attempts at reinvention, gin and its cocktail days were numbered; vodka sales would continue to climb throughout the 1960s. Vodka was ideal for the younger generation, which brought a less demanding palate to the table, as well as the desire to differentiate itself from past generations. Gin was perceived as old-fashioned and overly perfumed. In contrast, vodka has always been, by definition, neutral, a conduit, not a foundation. People quickly realized that it could get them drunk without an overt alcoholic taste. Women, in particular, liked the fact that it could not be noticed on the breath. With this profile on its side, vodka had overtaken gin as the most popular spirit in America by 1970. However, as history has shown, gin would not sit quietly in the shadows. In the early twenty-first century, it would rise to prominence yet again.

6

Gin's Renaissance

I'll stick with gin. Champagne is just ginger ale
that knows somebody.
Hawkeye Pierce, M*A*S*H

Today, gin and genever are experiencing a remarkable renaissance, perhaps more so than any other spirits. Since the turn of the millennium, more than 30 new gins have reached the marketplace. Old-school British distillers like Beefeater and Tanqueray have released modern takes on their classic products, while in the US numerous small-batch, artisan gins are being distilled with non-traditional botanicals. An American company has even stepped into the genever arena, making the first Dutch-style gin in the US. Not to be outdone, Great Britain has its own share of boutique distillers, whether those resurrecting defunct spirits like Old Tom or others simply inspired to create a new style.

The Dutch, despite their inherent ties to gin, have been less aggressive in their genever innovation. However, Bols has capitalized on the international interest in the old style, releasing a genever specifically targeted at and exported to the eager American and British markets.

Gin's Fall

The journey to regain its place in the spirits world has not been an easy one for gin. Up to the late twentieth century, the American gin industry, such as it was, offered but a few domestic brands, none of them noteworthy. Indeed, until the last decade the country had to rely on a slew of imports, mainly London Dry gins like Gordon's and Beefeater.

In the years following Prohibition, fanciful cocktails took a back seat to more pragmatic drinks – those with fewer ingredients and less fanfare. Along with the continued popularity of the Martini, Americans in the 1940s became acquainted with the gin and tonic, but because of the outrageous amount that bars charged for tonic water, the drink was seen as the domain of the upper crust. When tonic prices dropped, the

A present-day Bols Genever bottle. In response to the new cocktail culture particularly in the US, Bols makes this bottling just for the US and UK markets.

gin and tonic rose in popularity. In the early 1960s, the G&T would take on an aura of further sophistication since it was President John F. Kennedy's favourite tipple.

During the Second World War gin production was curtailed for the war effort. Despite the scarcity of real liquor, the military found creative ways to imbibe. In James Jones's novel *The Thin Red Line*, the soldiers mixed up a concoction 'rather like a Tom Collins', featuring Aqua Velva shaving lotion and grapefruit juice. PT boat crews were rumoured to drink straight 'torpedo juice', the alcohol used in the torpedo bays. The officers of the USS *Gunnel* were more fortunate. Challenged to a gin-drinking contest while making repairs in Scotland, the American officers soundly beat their British compatriots and were given a gin pennant, the British 'drinking flag', as a prize. The *Gunnel* proudly flew the green and white flag whenever the submarine made port.

The British distilleries were even harder hit during the Second World War. Like the American operations, they were commandeered by the military to make industrial alcohol. The resulting products were drolly referred to as 'Cocktails for Hitler'. Germany did not appreciate the humour. They bombed Goswell Road on 11 May 1941, crippling Gordon's entire operation. Remarkably, the workers returned to the distillery while the bombs were still being dropped in order to extinguish the incendiaries and finish the run for the next day's distillation. The Gordon's plant took years to rebuild; operations moved to Scotland and other locales during the reconstruction.

Plymouth fared better than Gordon's. In 1942, the Luftwaffe blitzed Blackfriars, but the distillery survived. In response to the attack, the Admiralty notified the entire British fleet. British officers stationed on Malta responded by offering a bottle of Plymouth to any gunner who sank a German ship or downed a plane.

Gordon's Export Gin shipping factory, *c.* 1930s.

When vodka rose to prominence in the 1960s and commanded the drink market in the 1970s, gin was viewed in both Britain and the US as a relic of a bygone era. In 1976, a subtle shift in the American public's view of alcohol began to coalesce. As part of his campaign, presidential candidate Jimmy Carter decried the businessmen's three-Martini lunch as an example of the results of unfair tax laws in which the rich were subsidized by the less wealthy classes. Carter won the election, and business people started rethinking their lunchtime drink selections.

As the 1980s arrived, the USA embraced a new mindset – addictive behaviour was under the spotlight, the exercise craze was just beginning and 'designer' water was the new cocktail. In a 1985 article, *Time* magazine proclaimed the Martini 'an amusing antique'.

Gin's Return

In 1987, a quiet revolution occurred within the spirits world with the launch of Bombay Sapphire London Dry Gin. Not only was the gin packaged in an attention-getting blue square bottle, but the bottle clearly declared the gin's ten botanicals, a major statement in the world of closely guarded gin recipes. The spirit's flavour profile offered more citrus than any London Dry gin before it; the move away from the typical pronounced juniper quality brought it an immediate following of non-gin drinkers. In no small manner, Bombay proved that gin could be reinvented. The revolution had begun but it would be another ten years before the spirits world would again see gin as a major player.

Bombay Sapphire London Dry Gin bottle. The distinctive blue glass with the major botanicals etched on the side was revolutionary.

While the UK has a history of producing super-premium gins, the USA does not. Fleischmann's, 'America's first gin', as their own advertising claims, is still produced in and for the US market; it does not position itself as competition for high-end imports. Seagram's, originally from Canada, is the USA's best-selling gin. And former British brands Gilbey's Gin and Booth's Gin are no longer produced in the UK but have a loyal following in the US, where they are now bottled.

Still, in comparison to both the traditional imports and the current American artisan gins, all of these are essentially 'bargain' brands. From the 1960s to the '90s, if a gin drinker wanted a more sophisticated tipple, he or she had to look to the London Dry imports.

Meanwhile, a new breed of bartender started to emerge. In 1970s London, while some discoed the night away and slurped Piña Coladas, a young Dick Bradsell studied the classic cocktails, championed fresh – not canned – ingredients, and went on to train an entire generation of aspiring British bartenders. Bradsell's equal in the USA was Dale DeGroff. Using Jerry Thomas's manual as his compass, DeGroff created a classic drinks menu in the 1980s at the Rainbow Room in New York. Thomas's recipes called for house-made syrups and fresh citrus, reflecting a sort of culinary perspective in drink preparation; DeGroff embraced the philosophy and customers quickly became believers.

The nostalgia for old-school cocktails spread, first with the 1990s swing culture – a younger generation fascinated by the movies, dance and music of the 1930s and '40s – then by the lounge crowd, which embraced the breezy irreverence of the Rat Pack. The dry gin Martini was king in those decades, so once again gin was moving into the spotlight.

According to the Gin and Vodka Association of Great Britain, exports of UK-produced gin (and vodka) increased by

Gordon's Gin advertisement, 1960s. The elegance and style represented in adverts like this one would inspire a new generation of gin drinkers in the 1990s.

more than 40 per cent from 1995 to 2000. This time period saw some interesting innovations in the use of botanicals and how they are distilled – steeped or vaporized, together or separately. There are actually over 200 botanicals that a distiller can use. The botanical triumvirate of the dry style traditionally consists of juniper, coriander and angelica. The other elements are what differentiate dry gins from one another.

It is the juniper that imparts a characteristic somewhat akin to fresh pine. This makes a gin 'dry', which essentially means unsweetened. The more juniper, the drier the gin. The addition of any sort of citrus, peel or otherwise, will create a fruitier, sweeter gin, thus not 'dry' in textbook terms. Coriander offers an elegant but powerful lemon-orange character without the sweetness imparted by true citrus and balances the juniper's headiness. The two flavours are then bound together with the addition of angelica, a slightly sweet, woody root that acts as a catalyst.

Beyond these three botanicals, a distiller could move in a spicy direction with cinnamon, ginger, cassia, cubeb pepper and grains of paradise. A more perfumed gin features elements like orris root or iris. The fruitier style brings citrus to the fore. Traditional London Dry gins and Dutch or Belgian genever will always be predominantly juniper-based because this is how their gins have always been made. And this is where the new gins began to differ markedly from the old, moving beyond juniper as their fulcrum and pursuing more non-conformist ingredients.

The secret to distilling gin is the way one extracts the essences of these botanicals. With London Dry and many other dry-style gins, the botanicals are macerated together and the mixture is steeped in the spirit for a specific period of time. London Dry must, by European Union definition, distil all the botanicals together, not in parts.

A selection of botanicals that might be used in gin (clockwise from top left): orange peel and lime, almonds, fennel seeds, cinnamon quills, nutmeg, juniper berries, coriander seeds, cardamom pods, cubeb berries.

Bombay Sapphire was the first gin to use vapour infusion in specially modified Carter Head stills. In this method, the botanicals are collectively held in individual copper baskets inside the still. The liquid spirit is converted to steam which passes through the botanicals creating a botanical-infused vapour, which then condenses into liquid spirit again. According to the company, this technique is more delicate than steeping, much like steaming vegetables instead of boiling them. It thus produces a subtle, balanced product.

The USA moved into the modern gin arena in 1998. The first of the premium, made-in-America gins was Junipero from the Anchor Distilling Company. Junipero gin did not try to reinvent the wheel, instead embracing the dry style and using classic botanicals. Where it differed noticeably was in its distinctly artisanal distillation method. Distilled by hand in a small copper pot still, rather than in mass market batches, Junipero set the bar for the flood of micro-distilleries to come. These distillers emphasized the handmade quality of their gin as the distinguishing feature.

Tanqueray, which has long held the number one spot amongst gin imported to the USA, is known for its powerful, juniper-forward nose and palate. In 2000, Tanqueray No. TEN arrived in the US, breaking all the rules of classic gin. Cleverly, it did not define itself as London Dry. Designed specifically for the American palate, No. TEN followed in Bombay Sapphire's footsteps with a lighter, more fruit-forward profile. The handpicked whole botanicals, which include white grapefruit, oranges and limes, are distilled separately, then redistilled with traditional 'dry' botanicals, as well as chamomile and fresh lime slices. This double distillation is what prevents No. TEN from calling itself London Dry. Regardless, the smooth, sweeter, citrus character brought instant success. In 2007, the brand would again capitalize on

Leopold American Small Batch Gin, one of the new artisanal gins.

the citrus element, releasing Tanqueray Rangpur, which high-lights the rare Rangpur lime.

Both Bombay and Tanqueray were established distillers; even Anchor had a long beer-brewing history in America. When an upstart by the name of Hendrick's, a new gin from Scotland, appeared, it truly kick-started the modern gin revo-lution. Launched in 2000 in the USA and 2003 in the UK, Hen-drick's purposely eschewed the traditional London Dry style and method. Using a combination of vapour infusion and steeping of botanicals, Hendrick's created a small-batch gin that was at once delicate and balanced. The utterly unortho-dox addition of cucumber and Bulgarian rose petals, as well as elderflower and chamomile, turned the concept of what gin should be on its head.

In essence, Hendrick's gave future distillers permission to experiment, subtly providing the encouragement for an entire crop of new, artisan producers. Not only have these

Some modern botanicals. Top row – poppy seed, chamomile flowers; middle row – cucumber, saffron threads (top), honeysuckle flowers (bottom), rose petals, tea leaves; bottom row – lavender buds, caraway seeds.

Aviation Gin, a new gin made in the Pacific Northwest and defined as a New Western Dry Gin.

gin-makers begun to explore unorthodox botanicals including various flowers and spices, but they are also using unique distilling methods – including cold distillation and distilling the botanicals in fractions – to produce gins of specific character.

With the plethora of new botanicals being used, the question of how to define these gins is problematic. Essentially, the majority of them are artisan products, in the sense that they are generally made in small quantities with more hands-on attention to each batch of spirits. In contrast, while companies like Gordon's, Tanqueray and Beefeater distil spirits of impeccable quality, they are large-scale operations designed to produce for mass markets. David Wondrich has used the term 'international style' to group the various gins that do not fall into the London Dry, Plymouth, Old Tom or genever categories.

One company, Aviation Gin, has chosen 'New Western Dry Gin' as its designation of choice. This definition requires that juniper still be the dominant botanical, but it allows great flexibility in the use of the 'supporting botanicals', thus creating a sort of 'artistic "flavor" freedom'. London Dry purists raise an eyebrow at this somewhat nebulous explanation, particularly as these various modern botanicals tend to add an inherent hint of sweetness to the gin. Still other gins, like Bluecoat out of Philadelphia, use the term 'American Dry Gin', which is simply a twist on the London Dry category.

Non-traditional Advertising

In 1980, Absolut Vodka unveiled its ground-breaking 'Absolut Perfection' campaign, which featured nothing but the bottle and the tag line. Since then, the company has produced hundreds of similarly themed ads, which feature an image or object shaped like an Absolut bottle and a complementary tag line. Many have been tailored for specific magazines such as the 'Absolut Centerfold' for *Playboy* magazine and the 'Absolut Cities' campaign for *Newsweek*. Certainly, Absolut reinvented the wheel with its eye-catching ads.

When Bombay Sapphire launched, it knew that it not only had to compete in this arena: it had to conquer. The company quickly aligned itself with the art world, suggesting a sort of rarefied, international style. For the ad campaigns, various designers created unique, sapphire-toned 'art' that complemented the blue Bombay bottle. Emma Gardner's blue paisley fabric, Tord Boontje's elaborate floral light design and Karim Rashid's cocktail glass have all been featured.

From the outset, Hendrick's positioned itself as an iconoclast. The tongue-in-cheek advertising campaign featured

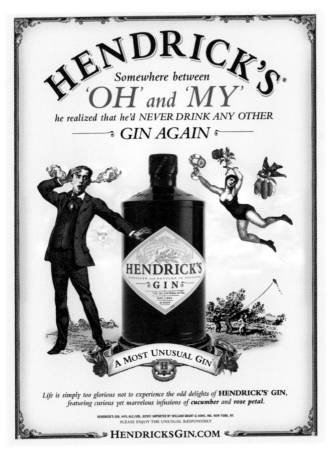

A modern Hendrick's Gin advertisement. The use of retro imagery conjures up a golden age of gin drinking.

Tanqueray Gin, *Tony Sinclair*, advertisement, 2005. The campaign was designed to appeal to a hipper generation of gin consumers.

Victorian men and women, often in mildly provocative situations with cucumbers. Like Bombay Sapphire, Hendrick's also set itself apart with a unique bottling style. The sturdy black glass apothecary container recalls a bygone era with its old-fashioned cork stopper and diamond-shaped label.

Martin Miller's Gin highlights the marriage of classic and modern with the focus on 'people who are looking for something new and authentic'. This idea is captured in the print ads which feature something old and something new – a proud husky and a pink poodle, a funky high-top sneaker and an oxford shoe, a leather couch and a 'lips' sofa – divided by a bottle of Martin Miller's gin.

Other companies employ edgy packaging. Bulldog Gin is made in the time-honoured London Dry style, but the bottle is a masculine matte grey with a spiked 'dog collar' on the bottle neck. Even the venerable Plymouth redesigned its original rounded bottle featuring the familiar distilling monk with a sleeker, modern style.

Of all the gin companies, Tanqueray is particularly emblematic of this search for a new audience. In 1994, rapper Snoop Dogg released his song 'Gin & Juice', referencing Seagram's ready-to-drink cocktails, which were specifically targeted at an urban market. Snoop also prominently mentioned Tanqueray by name in the song; the company seemed to take note. In 1999, Tanqueray retired their august and gentlemanly Mr Jenkins, an invented character employed in ads for five years. Then, in 2000, they released Malacca Gin, whose spicy, fruitier profile was targeted at the African-American market. Though Malacca gained an isolated following among gin connoisseurs, the brand was retired within a few years of release.

In 2005, Tanqueray launched its first US television commercials, featuring a suave young black man named Tony Sinclair. With his smooth British accent and coolly delivered 'Ready to

Tanqueray?' tagline, Sinclair was vastly different from Mr Jenkins and was clearly appealing to a younger, cooler, more ethnically diverse audience.

The Resurrection of Old Styles

Currently, a major shift in the gin world has occurred with the reintroduction, particularly to the American market, of pre-Prohibition-style genevers and sweetened gins, such as Old Tom. Long relegated to forgotten cocktail books, these gins are experiencing a resurgence in popularity for several reasons.

Over the last decade, there has been a major change in the way people view cocktails. This is due in great part to cocktailians like Dale DeGroff, Dick Bradsell and all the new mixologists who have followed their lead. Once bartenders started discovering classic drinks like those in Jerry Thomas's

A bottle of modern Ransom 'Old Tom' Gin, designed in an old-fashioned manner to reflect its heritage as one of the early gin styles.

famous guide, demand for the specific gins the recipes required rose accordingly.

For a number of years, people like DeGroff and David Wondrich quietly nudged various gin producers, making it quite clear that there was a receptive audience for these old world recipes. The barometer for how the cocktail culture had changed can be seen in the arrival of these resurrected gins.

Several versions of Old Tom, including Hayman's, Ransom and Jensen, have made it to the market. The Dorchester Hotel offers an exclusive one based on an eighteenth-century recipe, made for them by Hendrick's producer William Grant.

Sloe gin, a traditional homemade fruit liqueur, is available in Great Britain from Gordon's, Plymouth and Hayman's. Plymouth recently released it in the US as well. Made from sloe berries, sloe gin features in cocktails like the Sloe Gin Fizz. Plymouth also makes a damson gin, flavoured with damson plums.

In addition to Old Tom and fruit gins, genever is staging its own comeback. In 2007, Anchor Distilling released Genevieve 'Genever-Style' Gin, the first modern American-made genever. Soon after, Bols created a modern genever, specifically for the American and British markets. Intent on creating an authentic old-style genever, the bottling emphasizes the character of the malt wine, thus evoking the whisky-like element of true Dutch gin. And, in late 2011, the company released a new, barrel-aged genever that is aged for 18 months in French Limousin oak casks, resulting in an even more complex flavour profile.

Genever Young and Old

Ironically, the genever culture in the Netherlands and Belgium has not grown in the same ways as the gin culture of America and Britain. Since the 1950s, a bland, vodka-like genever

Old Schiedham Genever, available only at the Jenevermuseum in Schiedam, Netherlands. The recipe offers a very authentic expression of Old World genever.

classified as *jonge* has dominated the marketplace in both countries. In fact, in Holland, one brand of *jonge* genever outsells the entire vodka category, totalling over three million cases per year. *Jonge* denotes the lack of maltwine, not the age of the product. *Oude*, or old-style, genever – with a high malt wine content – can still be found, but it is drunk only by 'serious' imbibers. Two other specialized categories exist. *Korenwijn*, or corn-wine genever, must contain at least 51 per cent malt wine by law. While not governed by legal definitions, *moutwijnjenever*, or malt wine genever, generally has above 51 per cent malt wine; this is the style that Jerry Thomas used in his recipes, but it is incredibly scarce now.

Today, the truest expression of old-style genever can be found at the genever museum in Schiedam. There, they produce Old Schiedam Genever with 100 per cent malt wine, 40 per cent alcohol, and the judicious use of juniper as the only botanical. Further differentiating it, the genever is aged for three years in first-fill bourbon barrels. Other companies that make fine genevers include the small-scale producers Rutte and Zuidam.

In Belgium, the company that holds sway in the market, both in terms of quality and quantity, is Filliers, founded in 1880. Even so, genever's reputation has suffered since the turn of the century. Cheap alcohol led to over-indulgence and the identification of genever as being lower class. Field workers would start their morning with a bracing shot of genever, while factory workers often received their wages in the factory owner's cafe where they spent their money on drink.

Then, during the Second World War, the Nazi war machine confiscated the copper stills used in genever production to make ammunition. This, coupled with the 1919 Vandervelde Law, which prohibited the serving of distilled spirits in public places, was the death knell to the Belgian genever industry. Today, even in Belgium's genever capital of Hasselt, bars rarely

A political cartoon published by the Antwerp Union of Hotels, Barkeepers and Restaurants that made fun of the Vandervelde Law, c. 1919.

serve more than one type of *oude* genever. Along with international spirits like brandy and vodka, fruit genevers, essentially fruit-flavoured schnapps, are immensely popular among the new generation of drinkers, which has failed to embrace real genever to any great degree.

Recently, however, genever has been given protected status by the European Union, which has declared that genever can only be labelled and sold as such if it is made in Holland, Belgium, the Nord and Pas-de-Calais regions of France and the provinces of Nordrhein-Westfalen and Niedersachsen in Germany. More specifically, *jonge* and *oude* genever can only be labelled and sold as such in Holland and Belgium. Further, genever has been named as a component of the Slow Food Ark of Taste, which designates and seeks to protect food and drink that is 'endangered'.

The Rest of the World

Beyond the gin centres of Britain, the US, the Netherlands and Belgium, gin has a strong following in numerous other countries. The Philippines, the world's largest producer and consumer of gin, drinks nearly 50 million cases a year. Although there are few imported gins, Gilbey's used to sell 95 per cent of its annual production worldwide to the Philippines. The country's main brand is Ginebra San Miguel Premium Gin. Another brand is Gin Bulag. In Tagalog, the Filipino language, *bulag* translates as 'blind' or 'to blind someone', thus Gin Bulag equates rather dramatically to 'the gin that makes you blind'. Alcohol is an essential, if not the central, element of Filipino social life; friends often gather in front of their homes or on the streets to drink gin and tonic or gin and a still lemon-lime mixer, both less costly alternatives to straight gin.

Spain follows the Philippines in the world gin market and is the largest consumer in continental Europe. The major brand is Larios, whose packaging closely mimics that of Gordon's Gin. As the fourth-largest gin brand in sales worldwide, Larios is the basis for Gin Larios con Coca Cola, a combination that came about in the 1960s and continues to be popular today. Off the coast of Spain, on Menorca, Xoriguer Gin De Mahon is produced. A remnant of British colonialism, Xoriguer is the only gin aside from Plymouth that has its own geographic designation.

British colonialism was the major factor in India's burgeoning gin industry. Faced with an influx of gin-drinking foreigners, enterprising Indian companies started making their own gins. Today, gin is considered a more feminine drink, but both gin companies and bartenders are trying to change that perception. Distilled since 1959, McDowell's 'Blue Riband'

Gin Xoriguer de Mahon. The label features one of the windmills that dot the landscape of Menorca.

Gin accounts for approximately 50 per cent of the domestic gin market. Gilbey's Gin is distilled in India under licence; Bombay Sapphire Gin, Gordon's Gin and Beefeater Gin also have a presence.

In Eastern Europe, the home of vodka, gin shows up in surprising ways. In Russia, people consume Greenall's canned gin and tonic, known as Ready-To-Drink, on their way to work in the morning. The Polish have been drinking gin since Dutch sailors introduced it in the eighteenth century. The most popular brand produced in-country is Gin Lubuski, which also makes a Ready-to-Drink Lubuski Gin and Tonic.

In Uganda, the locals consume Waragi gin. The name is derived from 'war gin', a term used by British expatriates during the 1950s and '60s for the local alcohol called *enguli*. Waragi can be made from various local crops, including bananas and

One of the original London Dry brands, Greenall's, produces a popular canned gin and tonic, a new breed of ready-mixed cocktail to go.

sugar cane; it is often referred to as 'banana gin' and has a dissolute reputation, causing a great deal of alcoholism, and numerous deaths due to adulteration. In 2008, James Akena, a Lira Municipality Member of Parliament, demonstrated a more productive use for Waragi gin, which was combined with petrol to power a bicycle with a 500 CC engine. His hope was that the fuel amalgam could help the country's gasoline crisis.

Yesterday and Today

More than any other spirit, gin can incite an argument or elicit poetry. Whisky brings to mind the highlands of Scotland and whiskey, the dusky vales of Ireland; rum connotes pirates and the triangular trade; vodka speaks of steely Russian politicos and stark Siberian winters. All of these spirits have their own fascinating histories, but gin's history is truly a world history charting a path from the Middle East to Europe to America.

Since ancient times, gin's central component, juniper, has been used as a curative in the cultures of Egypt, Greece and Rome. During the time of the bubonic plague, juniper was the supreme panacea across Europe. When genever was developed in Holland, it became both a currency and a daily ration for the Dutch East India Company, whose members took it to places as diverse as Argentina and Indonesia.

In Great Britain, gin crossed social boundaries as the tipple of both the impoverished and the aristocrat. Like the Dutch, the British East India Company took gin with them as they colonized, spreading it to India and beyond. In America, gin – whether genever, Old Tom, London Dry or 'bathtub' – was intrinsic to the birth and evolution of the cocktail, more so than any other spirit. Modern gins from all corners of the globe – Sweden, New Zealand, America, Spain – speak to an

Bols 'Very Old Hollands' poster, designed in 1924 and used into the 1970s.

evolving international spirits culture that embraces innovation and experimentation.

One look at the past decade suggests that gin has reclaimed its central position in the drink world. Certainly, it offers a variety of styles unlike any other spirit. Traditional London Dry appeals to the classicist, who embraces its juniper-laden character. Vodka-lovers and those looking for something that makes them rethink gin will be rewarded by a foray into the new world of modern botanicals. And for those eager to take a journey back in time, the mellow sweetness of Old Tom or the whiskey-like intensity of *oude* genever provide a glimpse into and taste of drink history.

Regardless of one's tipple, gin requires a palate that embraces flavour, not a body that merely desires inebriation. It is a spirit whose rocky evolution parallels mankind's history, both lowly and noble. In the world of ardent spirits, gin is the most alchemical of all, able to transform two humble elements – grain and juniper – into an elixir of infinite complexity and reward.

Recipes

As with any mixed drink, the final product will only be as good as the ingredients that go into it. Most of these recipes call for a specific gin, or suggest one to use. It is worth experimenting with different gins in different drinks. Note that the conversion from American imperial measurements to international metric measurements is not exact.

Classic Cocktails

Corpse Reviver (No. 2)

Recipe reconstruction courtesy of Ted Haigh, author of
Vintage Spirits and Forgotten Cocktails. Originally from
The Savoy Cocktail Book (1930) compiled by Harry Craddock.

1 ounce (30 ml) fresh lemon juice
1 ounce (30 ml) Lillet Blanc*
1 ounce (30 ml) Cointreau
1 ounce (30 ml) dry gin
1 dash absinthe**

Shake well with ice and strain into a cocktail glass. Drop a stemless cherry into the bottom of the glass. As almost every modern version of this drink recipe will note, the ingredients *must* be measured exactly. (*The original recipe called for Kina Lillet, unavailable today.

Apertivo Cocchi Americano is a solid substitute. **Recommended absinthe: Marteau Absinthe de la Belle Epoque.)

Gin Cocktail

Adapted from Jerry Thomas's 1862 reprint of
How to Mix Drinks, or the Bon Vivant's Companion.

3 or 4 dashes of gum syrup*
2 dashes bitters**
2 ounces (60 ml) genever or genever-style gin
1 or 2 dashes curaçao
1 small piece lemon peel

Per Thomas's exact recipe, fill a cocktail shaker one-third full of fine ice, shake well and strain into a (cocktail) glass. (*For gum syrup, substitute simple syrup. To make: Heat 1 part superfine (icing) sugar in 1 part water until combined. Store in refrigerator. **Bitters may be Angostura, Fee Brothers or Peychaud's, per one's taste.)

The Martinez

Adapted from Jerry Thomas's 1887 reprint of
How to Mix Drinks, or the Bon Vivant's Companion.

2 dashes maraschino liqueur
1 ounce (30 ml) Old Tom gin
2 ounces (60 ml) sweet vermouth

Stir with ice and strain into a cocktail glass. Place a quarter slice of lemon in the glass. And per Thomas, 'If the guest prefers it very sweet add two dashes of gum (i.e., simple) syrup.'

Pink Gin/Gin & Bitters/Gin Pahit

The proportion of bitters and the manner in which
it is introduced to the gin or the glass varies. This version
is adapted from *Jigger, Beaker, and Glass* (1939)
by Charles H. Baker Jr.

4 or 5 dashes Angostura bitters
Gin: Old Tom or London Dry

Shake the Angostura into a stemmed cocktail glass. Per Baker: 'Tip
the glass like the Tower of Pisa and twirl it between thumb and
fingers. Whatever Angostura sticks to the glass through capillary
attraction is precisely the right amount.' Pour out any bitters that
do not cling. Fill the glass with gin.

Ramos Gin Fizz (aka New Orleans Fizz)

Courtesy of cocktail historian David Wondrich

This is the original, 'secret' recipe from Henry Charles Ramos, who
offered it to the public after Prohibition closed his bar. Because
of the ingredients, the drink requires much shaking. In 1915, Ramos
employed 35 'shaker men', each of whom shook a Fizz until his
arms tired and then he passed the shaker on to the next man in line.

1 tablespoon superfine sugar
3 or 4 drops (no more) orange flower water
juice from ½ lime
juice from ½ lemon
1½ ounces (45 ml) Old Tom gin*
1 egg white
1 half-glass of crushed ice
approximately 2 tablespoons rich milk or cream
a little (about an ounce) seltzer water **

Place all ingredients in a shaker. Per Ramos: 'Shake and shake and shake until there is not a bubble left but the drink is smooth and snowy white and of the consistency of good rich milk.' (*Plymouth Gin will also work. **Modern bartending suggests that one strain the drink into a tall Collins glass then add the seltzer after, giving it a quick stir.)

The Original Singapore Sling
Recipe adaptation courtesy of gaz regan, author/bartender.
Many versions exist; this one includes the ingredients
from the Raffles Hotel in Singapore.

2 ounces (60 ml) Beefeater Gin
½ ounce (15 ml) Cherry Heering
¼ ounce (7.5 ml) Benedictine
½ ounce (15 ml) Cointreau
2 ounces (60 ml) pineapple juice
¾ ounce (22.5 ml) fresh lime juice
2 dashes Angostura bitters
club soda

Shake all ingredients except for the club soda in an iced shaker. Strain into a tall, ice-filled Collins glass. Top off with club soda.

The Immortal Singapore Raffles Gin Sling
This version is adapted from *Jigger, Beaker, and Glass* (1939)
by Charles H. Baker, Jr, who describes the drink as
'a delicious, slow-acting, insidious thing'. He includes
directions for the original recipe, which used equal parts
of all ingredients; his version below is a bit drier.

2 ounces (60 ml) dry gin or Old Tom gin
1 ounce (30 ml) cherry brandy
1 ounce (30 ml) Benedictine
club soda, to taste

Shake well with ice. Strain into a small highball glass with ice in it. Top off with chilled club soda. Garnish with a spiral of lime.

The Small Dinger
This oddity is listed on the first page of Cuba's
Bar La Florida Cocktails 1935 reprint.

Given that the bar was known as 'the Cradle of the Daiquiri Cocktail' – rum, sugar, and lime – this gin drink is all the more intriguing.

1 ounce/ (30 ml) Gordon's Gin (their recommendation)
1 ounce (30 ml) (Cuban) Bacardi Rum, or other good quality light rum
½ ounce (15 ml) ounce grenadine
½ ounce (15 ml) fresh lime juice

Shake well with ice and strain into a cocktail glass.

The White Lady
Adapted from *The Savoy Cocktail Book*.

Both Harry Craddock and Harry MacElhone of Harry's American Bar in Paris have been credited with this drink.

¾ ounce (22.5 ml) fresh lemon juice
¾ ounce (22.5 ml) Cointreau
1 ½ ounces (45 ml) dry gin

Shake well with ice and strain into a cocktail glass.

Modern Cocktails

Bold, Bright, and Fearless
Courtesy of gaz regan

regan says: 'If you use the Bols genever in this cocktail, you'll be sipping a kind, gentle cocktail with a goodly dose of character, and if you're not a big fan of whiskey, the Bols version should suit you well. If you are truly 'Bold, Bright, and Fearless', though, and if you like a tot of whiskey every now and again, use Anchor Distillery's Genevieve to make this cocktail. The Genevieve version is quite a doozy.'

1½ ounces (45 ml) genever
½ ounce (15 ml) Cointreau
½ ounce (15 ml) pineapple juice
½ ounce (15 ml) fresh lemon juice
1 dash Angostura bitters
1 lemon twist, as garnish

Shake well with ice and strain into a chilled cocktail glass.

The Fitzgerald
Courtesy of Dale DeGroff, author of *The Essential Cocktail*

While working at the Rainbow Room, DeGroff was challenged by a customer to create an alternative to the summertime gin and tonic. This is his delicious answer – a twist on the Gin Sour.

1½ ounces (45 ml) gin
¾ ounce (22.5 ml) simple syrup
¾ ounce (22.5 ml) fresh lemon juice
2 dashes Angostura bitters
lemon wheel for garnish

Shake all ingredients with ice and strain into a rocks glass. Garnish with a lemon wheel.

Gowanus Club Gin Punch
Courtesy of David Wondrich

Wondrich calls this 'a loose – but not too loose – pastiche' of mid-nineteenth century fancy Gin Punch recipes, adapted for modern gin. (Leopold's Gin offers the ideal citrus-flavoured profile needed to make this drink come alive.)

For the Punch
3 lemons
2 ounces (50 g) superfine (caster) sugar
1 cup (250 ml) lemon juice, fresh squeezed, strained
½ cup (125 ml) rich pineapple syrup*
1 ounce (30 ml) yellow Chartreuse
1 litre bottle Plymouth Gin
1 quart (1 litre) green tea
seltzer water or club soda, to top off
mint leaves, garnish

For the Pineapple Syrup
2 pounds (1 kg) demerara or turbinado sugar
1 pineapple

Peel three lemons, trying to get as little of the white pith as possible (a swivel-bladed peeler works best here). Put the peels in a large bowl and muddle them with two ounces (50 g) of the sugar. Let this sit for an hour to bring out the oils. Add one cup (250 ml) fresh-squeezed, strained lemon juice and stir until the sugar has dissolved. Then add one-half cup (125 ml) rich pineapple syrup*, one ounce (30 ml) yellow Chartreuse, a litre bottle of Plymouth gin and a quart (1 l) of weak green tea (made by leaving three teabags in a quart of hot water for three minutes, removing them and letting the tea cool). Stir again, fish out the lemon peels and refrigerate the punch base for at least an hour.

*To make rich pineapple syrup:

Stir two pounds (1 kg) demerara or turbinado sugar into one pint (500 ml) water over a low flame until the sugar has dissolved. Let cool. Peel, core and cut a pineapple into approximately three-quarter inch cubes. Put the pineapple in a bowl, add enough syrup to cover, seal the bowl with plastic wrap and let it sit overnight. Then strain out the chunks (these can be reserved for punch garnish, if kept frozen), bottle the syrup and keep it refrigerated.

To serve, fill a gallon (4 l) punchbowl half way with ice cubes, pour in the punch base and add a litre of cold seltzer or club soda. Stir briefly and garnish with mint leaves, if you must garnish.

Genever Alexander

Courtesy of Philip Duff, gin/genever expert and
founder of door 74 (Amsterdam)

Per Duff: This is 'essentially a milk punch . . . bringing full, malty flavour to a rich creamy drink'.

1 ½ ounces (45 ml) old (*oude*) genever*
1 ½ ounces (45 ml) dark crème de cacao liqueur
2 ¼ ounces (67.5 ml) regular full-cream milk
¾ ounce (22.5 ml) rich sugar syrup

Shake all the ingredients very hard with cold, solid ice-cubes. Strain into a chilled cocktail glass. Rasp some 99 per cent cocoa-solids dark chocolate over the top. (*The higher the malt wine content the better. A *Korenwijn* is good, a 100 per cent malt wine genever even better. Do not use young, *jonge*, genever.)

Unusual Negroni

Courtesy of Charlotte Voisey, portfolio ambassador
with William Grant and Sons USA (Hendrick's)

1 ounce (30 ml) Hendrick's gin
1 ounce (30 ml) Aperol
1 ounce (30 ml) Lillet Blanc

Combine ingredients in a mixing glass with ice and stir. Strain into a cocktail glass. Garnish with an orange twist.

Martin Miller's Gin & Tonic Sorbet

2 cups (455 g) sugar
2 tablespoons confectioners' (icing) sugar
2 cups (500 ml) seltzer
Juice of 6 lemons, strained
2 cups (500 ml) tonic water
2 ounces (60 ml) Martin Miller's Gin

Bring the sugars, seltzer and lemon juice to a boil, stirring occasionally. Remove from heat. Stir in Martin Miller's Gin and tonic. Refrigerate until cold, and then chill to slush stage in an ice cream/ sorbet maker. Store in freezer.

If you don't have an ice cream/sorbet maker, transfer the mix to a shallow container, put into the freezer; stir with a fork once every hour for about five hours or until you arrive at slush stage.

Garnish with a mint sprig, scoop of lemon curd or some fresh lemon zest.

How to Make Sloe Gin

Courtesy of Hugh Williams, Master Distiller Emeritus
Gordon's/Tanqueray

In England, traditionally, sloes are picked after the first frost. They are then ripe and should be black rather than reddish in appearance. Many people prick their sloes with a pin, add sugar and gin and let it steep for far too long. This can be dangerous. Most fruit stones contain cyanide compounds and they can be leached into the product. Sloes are no exception.

Here's a better way that will extract flavour from the fruit more quickly, and cut out the laborious job of pricking the sloes. Put the sloes in the freezer for 24 hours or more. They should be completely frozen. Remove and pour into preserving jars. Cover with a high-strength, good-quality gin. Screw down lid tightly. (Pouring room temperature gin on frozen sloes will split the skins, increasing the extraction rate of sloe colour and flavour.)

For four weeks, turn over each jar daily: one day on its base, one day on its lid. At the end of this period, leaving the sloes in the jars, strain the liquor (steep) into a glass bottle and screw down a closure or cork. Green glass is preferable. On the sloes, add ¾ jar of cool boiled water or distilled water to each jar. Repeat the turn over process for two weeks. Don't worry, you are extracting some of the alcohol absorbed by the sloes, and there is still a little colour that will come out. It will look like a 'rosé' wine tint.

After two weeks, strain this liquor onto the original steep. Mix. Sweeten to taste. Some people prefer to drink sloe gin young, and it can be. Others prefer to leave it for a few months. The longer it is left, the closer it gets to having a plummy, port-type character. Its colour changes too as it matures and oxidizes.

Appendix:
A Selection of Gins Today

From the United Kingdom to the Philippines, from the Netherlands to United States, gin in all its many forms continues to enjoy popularity. However, the global gin renaissance now ensures that traditional and national brands share shelf space with a wide range of modern products.

Modern Dry Gins

Where classic London Dry or Dry gins (Beefeater, Gordon's, Greenall's, Tanqueray, Plymouth and the 1845 latecomer Boodles) are defined by a botanical focus on juniper, modern dry gins – while still employing juniper – playfully break the rules, both botanically and in terms of distillation.

Bulldog London Dry Gin (UK): A super premium brand made in London proper, this gin quadruple distils and triple-filters its spirit. Botanicals including poppy, dragon eye, lotus leaves and lavender create its unconventional profile, which is also reflected in the aggressive packaging.

Cadenhead's Old Raj Gin (Scotland): In a nod to Indian gins from the colonial era, Old Raj distils saffron to impart a slight straw hue and an exotic tasting note. Further, all the botanicals are first steeped for 36 hours in a combination of alcohol and water. Available at 110 and 92 proofs.

Cap Rock Organic Dry Gin (USA): This organic gin uses only 'whole' botanicals, including dried pink rosebuds and lavender buds. Using a pot still, the base distillate is sourced from organic wheat and apple spirit.

DH Krahn Gin (USA): Distilled in a Stupfler alembic pot still, this gin undergoes a multi-step maceration process to extract the essences and oils. After a single-pass distillation, each batch sits for three months in a steel barrel to further mellow it. Unusual botanicals like California grapefruit peel and Thai ginger add distinctness.

Junipero Gin (USA): Released back in 1998 by Anchor Distilling, this was the first of the new crop of gins. While still relying on juniper as the predominant botanical, Junipero has a subtle spiciness that comes from various proprietary ingredients. (Anchor also makes a genever-style gin.)

Martin Miller's Reformed London Dry (UK): This gin, named after its wealthy and famous founder, is made in England with traditional botanicals. It is then shipped to Iceland, where the soft, glacier-fed water of Selyri Springs reduces the spirit's proof, producing a smoother taste.

Oxley Classic English Dry Gin (Scotland): This is the first gin to use cold distillation, which employs no heating whatsoever. Rather, a vacuum reduces pressure and lowers the temperature in the still, vaporizing the spirit. A cold finger probe then converts the vapour back to spirit. The process produces no 'heads' or 'tails' – the impure parts of the alcohol – only the best portion, or 'heart', of the spirit. Oxley is the only brand to use Scottish juniper berries, harkening back to the seventeenth century, when Scottish berries were imported for Dutch genever.

Whitley Neill Gin (UK): Distilled in an antique copper pot still, this gin uses African baobab fruit pulp and Cape gooseberries, neither of which has been used in gin distillation before. Still, juniper and other traditional spices make for a dry character.

Modern Artisan/International/New Western

Many of the modern gins have chosen the path of Hendrick's, visibly and successfully flaunting convention. While juniper often still plays a role, surprisingly new flavours dominate here. Even a number of those in the London Dry style are toying with formulas.

Aviation Gin (USA): The company classifies itself by the self-titled moniker 'New Western Dry Gin'. While juniper is essential, other botanicals are permitted and encouraged. Aviation focuses on floral, savoury notes found in elements like lavender, Indian sarsaparilla and anise seed.

Beefeater 24 Gin (England): From the established London Dry house, this gin takes the original recipe as a base then adds a blend of rare Japanese Sencha and Chinese green teas as well as grapefruit peel. These are soaked with the traditional botanicals, including juniper, in Beefeater's unique 24-hour (hence the name) steeping process.

Bloom Gin (UK): Created by the industry's only female distiller, Bloom is triple-distilled and batch-produced using distinctive 'country garden' botanicals including chamomile, honeysuckle and pomelo. Reflecting Bloom's old-school parent company Greenall's, juniper is still at the centre of the mix.

Caorunn Gin (Scotland): A brand that reflects true regionalism, this gin uses Highland water and Celtic botanicals, including rowan berries, dandelion, heather, Coul Blush apple and bog myrtle.

G'Vine Floraison and G'Vine Nouaison (France): G'Vine uses Ugni Blanc grapes as the base spirit instead of grain. As with brandy, the grapes are made into wine first then distilled four times into neutral grape spirit. The gin features a remarkably different botanical – the green grape flower, which blooms for only a few days per year. This flower is harvested and macerated in the spirit then combined with nine other traditional, whole-fruit botanicals, including juniper, nutmeg and cubeb berries.

Leopold's American Small Batch Gin (USA): This small-batch gin from Colorado adds the botanicals (including cardamom, coriander, Valencia oranges and pomelos) in fractions, which means that each is distilled separately and then combined as a whole in order to emphasize the individual flavours. As with high-end whisky, this gin uses only the 'hearts' of the distillation, resulting in a cleaner overall character.

No. 209 Gin (USA): Juniper plays a secondary role to Bergamot oranges and hand-sorted cardamom. Water from the Sierra Nevada Mountains is blended with botanicals soaked overnight in neutral spirit. The company specifically refers to its product simply as 'gin', hoping to distinguish itself from the London Dry style.

Right Gin (Sweden): The use of North American corn as the grain base adds a sweetness to this gin, while the citrus notes take precedence to the juniper. Soft water is sourced from a lake near Malmo, Sweden; Sarawak black pepper is an uncommon botanical addition.

Small's Gin (USA): This handmade gin is created in small-pot batches and sources naturally farmed, wild-grown botanicals, including star anise, caraway and raspberries. The master recipe is culled from a combination of various nineteenth-century gin recipes. (Small's producer Ransom Spirits also makes an Old Tom gin.)

Old Tom Gin

According to David Wondrich, the term 'Old Tom' covers a vast multitude of gins from a historical perspective. These include everything from the catch-all term for eighteenth-century gin to early nineteenth-century genever-style sweetened gin to late nineteenth-century sweetened dry gin. Today, only a few producers are even attempting to replicate or recreate these old recipes.

Hayman's Old Tom Gin (UK): This slightly sweet, rounded evocation of the style is based on the company's own recipe from the late 1800s. The botanicals include familiar ones such as juniper, coriander, angelica, orris root and citrus. It was the first Old Tom to reach the American market.

Ransom Old Tom Gin (USA): Developed in collaboration with cocktail historian David Wondrich, this is the first Old Tom made in the United States. It is vastly different from Hayman's as it owes more to early – not late – nineteenth-century recipes. Its soft amber colour results from barrel ageing; the subtle, malty notes carry an underlying juniper character and the sweetness comes only from the botanicals, not any additional sugar, as was historically the case.

Jensen's Old Tom Gin (UK): In addition to Hayman's in Britain, this Old Tom is based on a recipe from the 1840s. The natural sweetness comes from a high proportion of botanicals, which include juniper at the fore, as well as floral and citrus notes. (Jensen's also produces their Bermondsey Gin, which is in the old, dry style.)

Genever and Genever-style Gins

The Netherlands and Belgium continue to produce genever, although theirs are not exported to the United States. Instead, the growing American interest in genever has led the Dutch company Bols and the American producer Anchor Distilling to cater directly to the us market.

Genevieve 'Genever-Style' Gin (USA): The first modern American-made genever, Genevieve uses the same proprietary botanicals as Junipero Gin, also a product of Anchor Distilling.

Bols Genever (Holland): In the model of an old-style genever, this newer product is distinctly whisky-like with a pronounced malt wine character. Four different distillates – malt wine (rye, wheat, corn), neutral grain spirit, juniper berry distillate and botanical distillate – are made separately, then blended.

Filliers Genever (Belgium): Still employing original nineteenth-century production methods, the company uses a traditional corn, rye and barley mixture.

Old Schiedam Genever (Holland): Today, the truest expression of old-style genever can be found at the genever museum in Schiedam. Their recipe uses 100 per cent malt wine and is 40 per cent alcohol with the judicious use of juniper as the only botanical. Further differentiating it, the genever is aged for three years in first-fill bourbon barrels.

Zuidam Genever (Holland): The former master distiller for DeKuyper works with his son to create this triple-distilled genever. The base grains are equal parts malted barley, corn, and rye; the botanicals, which include juniper, liquorice root, whole vanilla beans and marjoram, are added in the final, fourth distillation.

Select Bibliography

Boothby, William T., *Cocktail Boothby's American Bar-Tender* [1891], with a foreword by Fritz Maytag and David Burkhart (San Francisco, CA, 2009)

Broom, Dave, *Spirits and Cocktails* (London, 1998)

Coates, Geraldine, *Classic Gin* (London, 2000)

—, *The Mixellany Guide to Gin* (London, 2009)

Cooper, Ambrose, *The Complete Distiller* (London, 1757)

Dillon, Patrick, *Gin: The Much-Lamented Death of Madam Geneva* (Boston, MA, 2003)

Gately, Iain, *Drink* (New York, 2008)

George, M. Dorothy, *London Life in the Eighteenth Century* (New York, 1965)

Grimes, William, *Straight Up or On the Rocks* (New York, 2001)

Haigh, Ted, *Vintage Spirits and Forgotten Cocktails* (Gloucester, MA, 2004)

Haydon, Peter, *An Inebriated History of Britain* (Gloucestershire, 2005)

Jerry Thomas' Bar-Tender's Guide [1887], with an introduction by Ross Bolton (New York, 2008)

Kinross, Lord, *The Kindred Spirit* (London, 1959)

Lucia, Salvatore P., ed., *Alcohol and Civilization* (New York, 1963)

Okrent, Daniel, *Last Call* (New York, 2010)

regan, gaz, *The Bartender's Gin Compendium* (Bloomington, IN, 2009)

The Savoy Cocktail Book [1930], originally compiled by Harry Craddock with additions by Peter Dorelli (London, 1999)

Thomas, Jerry, *How to Mix Drinks or The Bon Vivant's Companion* [1862] (New York, 2009)

Van Schoonenberghe, Eric, *Jenever in de Lage Landen* (Bruges, 1996)

Warner, Jessica, *Craze* (New York, 2003)

Webb, Sidney, and Beatrice Potter Webb, *The History of Liquor Licensing in England Principally from 1700 to 1830* [1903] (Charleston, SC, 2008)

Wondrich, David, *Imbibe!* (New York, 2007)

Websites and Associations

Gin History and Brands

www.gintime.com

Tales of the Cocktail
(annual spirits convention in New Orleans)
www.talesofthecocktail.com

Museums

National Genever Museum Hasselt, Belgium
www.jenevermuseum.be

National Genever Museum Schiedam, Netherlands
www.jenevermuseum.nl

House of Bols Museum
www.houseofbols.com

Museum of the American Cocktail, New Orleans, Louisiana
www.museumoftheamericancocktail.org

Spirits Associations

Beverage Testing Institute (USA)
www.tastings.com

Distilled Spirits Council of the United States
www.discus.org

Gin and Vodka Association (UK)
www.ginvodka.org

Cocktail Recipes and Mixology Information

www.ardentspirits.com

www.cocktaildb.com

www.diffordsguide.com

Acknowledgements

Writing a book is a bit like mixing a drink. The finished product is only as interesting as the quality of the ingredients. I was fortunate to have remarkable 'ingredients' – a group of gin geniuses, who enthusiastically and tirelessly answered my questions, referred me to one another, sent images and drink recipes, and generally kept me honest. Dale DeGroff truly deserves the title 'King Cocktail'. He put me in touch with historian David Wondrich, ever ready with the smallest detail, and Ted Haigh, who endlessly provided whatever I asked of him (and I asked a lot). Ted introduced me to Hugh Williams, Master Distiller Emeritus of Gordon's/Tanqueray/Gilbey's. Hugh is not only a font of information about English gin, but a charming observer of life. Bartender, drinks consultant, and saloonkeeper Philip Duff was my genever 'Virgil'; Philip's vast knowledge was complemented by that of Henry Reymen at the Nationaal Jenevermuseum Hasselt, Guido Beauchaz at the Jenevermuseum Schiedam, and historian Ton Vermeulen at Bols. Brian Rea and gaz regan are cocktail royalty as well. In the scholarly arena, Jessica Warner was invaluable in researching the Gin Craze; Susan Walker of the Yale Library and Ken Albala at University of the Pacific helped track down vital documents; Colin Brewer, Dan Malleck, James Nicholls, Judy Stove, and Dave Trippel of the Alcohol and Drugs History Society provided much direction. In the world of 'the brands', I must thank a large group – Plymouth ambassador Simon Ford, Miranda Hayman of Hayman Brothers,

Charlotte Voisey of William Grant and Sons (Hendrick's), Diageo archivists Alia Campbell, Christine McCafferty, and Joanne McKerchar; Scott Leopold of Leopold Brothers Gin, Ryan Magarian of Aviation Gin, and Tad Seestedt of Ransom Spirits; G&J Greenall's Cathryn Zommer, Martin Miller's Lindsay Gorton and Bombay Sapphire's Danielle Katz. Thank you to publisher Michael Leaman and series editor Andy Smith for letting me play the gin game. And to my Reaktion editor Martha Jay and photo researcher Susannah Jayes for teaching me the rules. To paraphrase FDR, I think now would be a good time for a drink. Cheers.

Photo Acknowledgements

The author and the publishers wish to express their thanks to the below sources of illustrative material and/or permission to reproduce it:

Author's collection: pp. 80, 95; Aviation Gin: p. 125; Courtesy of Blue Island Ltd: p. 135; Collection of Lucas Bols: pp. 36, 37, 114, 138; Bombay Sapphire Gin: p. 117; © The Trustees of the British Museum, London: pp. 51, 52, 58, 67; Courtesy of Diageo: pp. 12, 62, 71, 74, 78, 100, 116, 119, 128; Getty Images: p. 21; William Grant & Sons: pp. 10, 15, 127; Courtesy of G&J Greenall's: p. 136; Collection of Ted Haigh: pp. 28, 70, 87, 91, 96, 97; Hayman's Gin: p. 69; Istockphoto: p. 6 (Sean Davis); Jenevermuseum, Hasselt, Belgium: pp. 11, 29, 30, 39, 133; Jenevermuseum, Schiedam, The Netherlands: p. 132; Leiden University Libraries: p. 25; Leopold Brothers: p. 123; London Metropolitan Archives: p. 44; US National Library of Medicine, Bethesda, Maryland: pp. 9, 17, 18, 20, 33, 38, 55, 56, 83, 99; Museum of the American Cocktail, New Orleans: p. 102; Plymouth Gin: pp. 63, 79; Ransom Spirits: p. 130; Collection of Brian Rea: p. 90; Sazerac Company: p. 93; David Solmonson: pp. 121, 124; Courtesy of Tikitnet: p. 110; Courtesy of the Lewis Walpole Library, Yale University: pp. 8, 42; Worshipful Company of Distillers: p. 43.

Index

italic numbers refer to illustrations; **bold** to recipes.